THE DEVELOPMENT OF HOUSING IN SCOTLAND

THE DEVELOPMENT OF HOUSING IN SCOTLAND

DOUGLAS NIVEN

CROOM HELM LONDON

© 1979 Douglas Niven
Croom Helm Ltd, 2-10 St John's Road, London SW11

British Library Cataloguing in Publication Data

Niven, Douglas
    The development of housing in Scotland.
    1. Housing policy – Scotland
    301.5′4′09411   HD7335.A3

    ISBN 0-7099-0159-3

Printed in Great Britain by
Biddles Ltd, Guildford, Surrey

CONTENTS

Illustrations

Acknowledgements

Introduction   11

1. Historical Background   13

2. Housing in Scotland, Housing in Europe   32

3. Housing in Scandinavia   48

4. Housing in the Public Sector   68

5. Priorities, Facts, Figures and Numbers   84

6. Housing in the Private Sector   96

7. Architects, Planners and Builders   103

8. Housing Societies and Associations   116

9. Possibilities for the Future   124

Index   132

ILLUSTRATIONS

1. Tenements at Hyndland, Glasgow. Architects: John McKellar and C.J. McNair.
2. The Study, Culross.
3. Terraced Housing at Delft, Holland. Architect: Herman Hertzberger.
4. Flats at Otaharju near Helsinki, Finland. Architect: Heikki Kaija Siren.
5. Terraced Housing at Moss Park, Glasgow. Architect: Glasgow Council.
6. Mixed Development at Cowcaddens, Glasgow. Architects: Walter Underwood & Ptrs.
7. Private Housing at Marly Green, North Berwick. Architect: Calthorpe and Mars. (Photograph by Inglis Stevens.)
8. Great Western Terrace, Glasgow. Architect: Alexander Thomson.
9. Flats at Comiston, Edinburgh. Architect: James Gray.
10. Flats and Maisonettes at Bridgend, Perth. Architects: James Parr & Ptrs.
11. Proposed Urban Renewal at Raeberry Street, Woodside, Glasgow. Student: Tommy Thomson, Tutor: Douglas Niven.

ACKNOWLEDGEMENTS

I should like to thank the many individuals and organisations in Scotland who helped to provide information for this study. My thanks are also due to Professor F.M. Martin of the Department of Social Administration at Glasgow University for his encouragement and advice.

Finally, I acknowledge the generous support given to the study by the Joseph Rowntree Memorial Trust, and in particular to the help given me by the Director, Mr Lewis E. Waddilove.

Douglas Niven,
Mackintosh School of Architecture,
University of Glasgow,
Glasgow.

INTRODUCTION

The Scottish housing problem is legendary; created mainly by the Industrial Revolution, its origins lie far back in the country's social, political and economic history. It is important to note that Scotland has never enjoyed a coherent, appropriate or particularly humane housing policy. In the recent past undue emphasis on public sector housing has distorted Scottish housing programmes and so restricted all other forms of housing tenure that many Scots now expect local authorities to act as the principal supplier of housing, and believe that they have little choice in the matter of how they are housed and where they live. Priority given to the number of local authority house completions between 1950 and 1970 to the exclusion of many other important considerations and suitable alternatives can now be regarded as a short-sighted policy and represents, in physical terms, a poor investment for the future.

Much has already been written on the nature and condition of Scottish housing since the report by the Royal Commission published in 1917 first drew attention to severe overcrowding and poor living conditions in the rural and urban areas of Scotland. A number of excellent publications have been written on the subject, particularly those issued on behalf of the Scottish Housing Advisory Committee; these publications, however, have limited application in that they tend to deal with specific problems and do not necessarily give lay people an opportunity to take a broad view of housing affairs, or to comprehend some of the bewildering ramifications which bedevil Scottish housing today. Official explanations by politicians, civil servants and government experts are of necessity rarely objective and often lead only to further confusion in the mind of the general public.

There are a number of surprising omissions in the existing published material on Scottish housing: for example, few comparisons have been made between Scottish housing policies and programmes and those which are carried out in other parts of the world. This applies particularly to Europe and Scandinavia. An independent observer might conclude, with some justification, that recent Scottish housing programmes had been devised in total isolation and without making reference to housing activities in the rest of the world.

Since 1950, private builders have made a very modest contribution to

Scottish house-building programmes. This section of the Scottish building industry apparently prefers to keep a low profile and sees little necessity for documentation and publication. Not much is known about the workings of the private sector and very little seems to have been written on the subject.

The problems faced by housing designers in Scotland has never received much publicity. Housing design is currently inhibited by a stultifying administrative and technical bureaucracy both at local and national levels which has nearly succeeded in stifling creative housing design in Scotland. This does not excuse the abysmal standard of design which has characterised so many housing developments in the recent past — that is another story.

Little is also known about the potential of the voluntary housing movement in Scotland. Housing associations and housing co-operatives have formed a vital 'third arm' to housing programmes in Europe and Scandinavia for many years. The movement is only now beginning to make a significant contribution to Scottish housing programmes; until comparatively recently, successive British governments have either ignored or given little support to these organisations in Scotland.

This study presumes to give an over-view of Scottish housing including the aspects mentioned above and also takes an 'un-official' look at the public sector. It is hoped that the book will give some insight into past and present housing problems and that it may stimulate further and more detailed study; it may even give policy makers and administrators an incentive to think more positively and humanely on housing matters in the future.

1   HISTORICAL BACKGROUND

I

Social and economic conditions altered rapidly and dramatically in
Scotland during the nineteenth century. The Industrial Revolution
came early to the country; the pace and rate of change was faster,
cruder and more concentrated over a smaller area than in England.
Inadequate provision was made for housing expanding populations in
newly created industrial areas; gross overcrowding was the sickening
by-product of successful industrial expansion in Victorian Scotland.
Acute social problems were created during this period which still cast
a blight on Scottish life in the latter half of the twentieth century.

Other factors, apart from the effects of the Industrial Revolution,
have had considerable bearing on the condition and nature of Scottish
housing, and these must not be overlooked in any historical summary
of housing in Scotland.

Agriculture still formed the basis of the Scottish economy at the
beginning of the eighteenth century. Nearly three quarters of the population, which at that time was about a million people, gained their
livelihood directly from the land, following methods of cultivation
favoured since medieval times. Antiquated farming techniques, agricultural blight and a wholly unreliable climate led to recurring crop
failures creating a fear of famine in many rural communities throughout
Scotland.

During the previous century prolonged periods of political and
religious strife had also created distress and uncertainty throughout the
countryside. In these trying circumstances there was little incentive for
country people to build substantial or permanent dwellings and this
was reflected in the 'farmtoun' settlements, which were scattered around
the countryside at the turn of the century. Houses within these settlements were described by a contemporary historian as 'crudely constructed shelters of dry stone walling, built without mortar, with branches or
rough spars for the roof and proofed against the elements with straw
and turf'. The floors of the buildings were often bare earth, the windows
were small, with little or no glazing and many had no chimney or proper
fireplace. A typical settlement consisted of six or more such dwellings,
each having its own kailyard, stackyard and midden; these were set in
no particular order or pattern upon a treeless landscape. The surrounding

land was divided into 'run-rig' or narrow strip fields and ground was set
aside for common grazing.

Ownership of the land in Scotland had largely passed into Norman
hands by the middle of the twelfth century; Normans found favour
with Malcolm Canmore and also David I. Apart from owning most of
the land, Normans held many of the chief offices in church and state.
A Norman aristocracy was established, and rapidly introduced Norman
habits, ideas and culture into Scotland. As a result, the old Scottish
feudal system, which moderated the possession of land by ancient bonds
of kinship and tribalism, was superseded by Norman feudalism which
embodied a much more rigid form of land tenure. Under this system all
land was held by the king; all occupiers of land became tenants of a
lord, who in turn was a tenant of the king. The lord's tenancy was
hereditary; the extent of a man's tenancy also determined his civil and
political rights. The precedents created by this ancient feudal code,
particularly in respect of land and property, still exert a strong influence
on Scottish affairs; ownership of land is critical in all forms of development now, as it was when the pattern of land ownership was first established by the heirs of Malcolm Canmore. The creation of a feudal
system based on the Anglo-Norman code, together with the imposition
of strong government and the reform of the existing church enabled
David I to 'form a nation' from many groups of disunited peoples
throughout Scotland.

The king was also responsible for the formation of new townships in
the countryside. These early essays in town planning were instituted to
preserve the power of the crown, to promote social stability and to
create points of economic expansion. Townships, created by royal
decree, became known as 'Royal Burghs' to distinguish them from the
later creations of the Lords of Scotland, which were simply known as
'Burghs of Barony'. In the Royal Burghs, people were encouraged to
establish settlements beside existing or newly formed fortifications. In
return, they were granted privileges, which included the special right to
trade abroad. The burghs also enjoyed considerable autonomy and even
extended their controlling influences into the surrounding countryside.

By the end of the twelfth century more than twelve 'Royal Burghs'
had been created. The Burghs of Ayr, Aberdeen, Dumfries, Inverness,
Perth, were all formed at strategic crossing-points to large rivers. Edinburgh, St Andrews and Stirling were enlarged from existing townships
which had been associated with ancient castles. Forres and Elgin in the
north, Linlithgow in Lothian, Lanark in Clydesdale and Jedburgh and

Peebles in the Borders were constructed beside newly formed defensive strong-points.

Most burghs originated with a single main street, usually known as the High Street or 'Hie Gait'. Where the burgh was associated with a castle, the principal street was set axially to the fortification, and terminated at a main gateway or 'Port'. Towards the middle of the street stood the town house or Tolbooth and the Market Cross, which symbolised the authority of the burgh. Some layouts also offered a secondary main street which ran parallel to the main street.

From the earliest times, each inhabitant had a 'land' or 'tenement' with a 'frontage', or house constructed in timber, to the main street or secondary street. The tenement stretched back in the form of a narrow strip terminating at the secondary street in the case of an inner holding, and at the town walls or dykes in the case of an outer building. The 'lands' closely resembled the narrow strip fields or 'run-rigs', which were commonly associated with the 'farmtoun' settlements of the period. On the 'frontage' a house was built of one, then later of two, three or four storeys, leaving the remainder of the site to be used for cultivation and other purposes.

With the increase in population and a restricted amount of building space within the burgh enclosure, other houses came to be erected on the 'lands' behind the 'frontage' house. A 'pend' or archway was formed under the frontage house, leading to a series of courts and closes, which in turn gave access to houses at the back. These properties became known as the 'backlands' of the burgh.

Many of the early burghs, which had been built initially in timber, were reconstructed in stone during the sixteenth and seventeenth centuries. Several new Burghs of Barony were also erected by a number of enterprising noblemen along the Fifeshire coast to support a new fishing industry, or to handle an increasing trade in coal and salt with Dutch and Baltic ports. These little burghs, such as Culross and Crail, still provide fragmentary examples of an indigenous domestic architecture of rare quality.

It is thought that the first inhabitants of the new burghs were chosen from some of the more desirable elements in the 'feudal pyramid'. These persons, once established, chose future burghers with considerable care, restricting access to the merchants and trades guilds by a lengthy period of graduating membership. A social 'pecking order' most certainly existed in the burghs at this time, but relationships between neighbours were closely interwoven, and many enjoyed the mutual respect of their fellows regardless of position or rank.

II

The first half of the eighteenth century brought few alterations to building development in Scotland. Edinburgh and Stirling were still the principal centres of population; both communities were still contained within the old town walls or fortifications. Development tended to rise upwards, in keeping with the tall narrow vertical style of contemporary towns in Northern Europe. Houses achieved an astonishing height of ten storeys in Edinburgh. Many were divided into flats at each storey height and connected to the street by a narrow and steep turnpike stairway. The 'backlands' were extensively built over by this time to meet the needs of an increasing population.

According to contemporary historians, social life in this community was both interesting and varied. Families of all ranks lived in the close proximity of the same tenement; peers, lords of session, clergy, doctors, shopkeepers and artisans lived at varying levels up the same access stair, while the watercaddy, sweep and chairman lodged in the cellars or the attics. Incomes were small, tastes were simple; the gap between rich and poor was not at this time decisively obvious. A highly mixed and diverse group of people had come together through economic necessity and mutual protection, to form a tightly packed community clustered along a ridge between the Castle and Holyrood Abbey.

It is significant that the wealthier citizens escaped from the problems created by high density, poor sanitation and the general squalor of the old burgh at the first opportunity. Examples set by London and other continental towns and a general raising of economic standards at home fostered a desire for improvement among the more enterprising burghers. At this time, a group of leading citizens decided to prepare a lengthy report on the physical condition of Edinburgh; in this they recommended, among other things, the construction of a 'new town' on a ridge to the north of the old burgh. It was suggested that the burgh council be made responsible for the over-all co-ordination of the project, and that a planning competition be held to determine a suitable plan for the first phase of development. This excellent proposal was sanctioned by the council and, in due course, a winner chosen from a small number of competitors.

The disarmingly simple layout plan by the winner, James Craig, is already too well known to warrant detailed description here; the execution of his plan by a series of famous and not so famous architects has also been well documented by others and, likewise, bears little repetition. What must be emphasised, however, was the tenacity of purpose displayed by the developers. In the face of many difficulties, their enlightened promotion of the project inspired both architects and builders to create one of the finest examples of Georgian domestic architecture in Europe.

The promoters of the new town may, or may not, have appreciated that the new development would have a profound effect on the closely knit social fabric of the old burgh. As the houses were completed, it became obvious that only the wealthy could afford to take up residence in the 'new town'. A few houses were built to accommodate skilled tradesmen, but the number of these constructed was small in proportion to the rest. Therein, it may well be argued, lay the fundamental weakness of the 'new town' concept. The re-creation of the old community of the High Street in more congenial and decorous surroundings did not appear to concern the promoters. The burgh council might also have resisted the temptation to build on a grand scale, creating instead a new-town form in which the welfare of the community as a whole was considered and accommodated. But this was really too much to expect; the moving spirits of the age had their eyes set upon a grand design and chose instead to build a series of domestic monuments for a minority of the citizens of Edinburgh.

III

Between 1730 and 1830 a total change took place in the methods of husbandry employed in Scotland. The old run-rig and joint-tenancy system was discontinued and the enclosure of common land was 'legally' undertaken. 'Farmtoun' settlements were broken up and their 'owners' were discouraged from building houses, however temporary, in the countryside.

The first capitalist farmers emerged; marshes and bogs were drained and trees planted. A smaller proportion of the population occupied the land, but this group was now able to produce a surplus in farm products. The disposal of surplus crops and animals without sophisticated means of transportation obviously created problems. According to contemporary thinkers, the solution lay in the creation of village communities; a village would provide a point of consumption for the produce from the surrounding areas and also give employment to a proportion of persons displaced by the reorganisation of the land.

The idea of creating village communities was inspired by a curious amalgam of economic, social and aesthetic motives. Instinctively, local landowners realised that organised rural communities gave them greater control over local populations. Many of the new villages, especially those constructed after 1770, were well planned, soundly constructed and some are of lasting architectural value.

Early examples of these model village developments were situated at

Crieff, laid out to a grid plan by the Duke of Perth from 1731 onwards, the village of Ormiston in East Lothian, created by John Cockburn about 1740, and much admired by contemporary writers, and Inveraray, reconstructed by the Duke of Argyll after 1742. The latter is a fine example of Scottish rural architecture and serves as a lasting memorial to aristocratic patronage. Of the others, Granton, Fochabers, Falkland and Kirkcudbright come most readily to mind. These planned villages were founded on an economic base of agriculture, fishing, rural industry or factory industry. Landowners often took great pains to attract industrialists to set up and to manage new industry in their newly formed communities. Almost all villages were built of stone which was some-times rendered or whitewashed; most had roofs of tile or slate; many consisted of two storeys; some even had between three and five rooms to a dwelling. While some of these villages became thriving communities, others failed, especially those which were based on rural industry. This was due to technical innovation in adjoining towns, improved methods of transportation and shifting patterns of trade within the country.

Several factory villages were established between 1780 and 1800 in various parts of the country where water-power could be harnessed to drive machinery. These settlements differed from the traditionally plan-ned village, in that the landowner no longer controlled the detailed development; this was left to an industrialist who had greater technical know-how and expertise in raising capital for industrial innovation.

A number of these industrialists made it their business to provide reasonable housing for their work people. A contemporary writer des-cribes the Ballikinrain mill in Stirlingshire as surrounded by sturdy two-storey houses with slate roofs and laid out to a regular and neat plan. Deanston and Stanley in Perthshire, Catrine in Ayrshire were also well laid out and provided good housing accommodation for the work people. The most famous example of all, at New Lanark, was first developed by David Dale, a well-known Glasgow businessman, then later enlarged by his son-in-law, Robert Owen. The management of these communities— particularly the New Lanark complex — was unquestionably paternalistic both in attitude and character, and frequently the motive behind the venture was suspected and frowned upon by contemporary industrial-ists. But at least they provided decent housing for the work people, which is more than can be said for many of their industrial successors in the nineteenth century.

IV

Steady progress in linen manufacture, and the coal and iron industries was made in Scotland during the period 1760 to 1820. New developments in banking also accompanied this expansion. Further technical progress by 1800 led to the development of a mechanised cotton industry in the existing townships of the Clyde valley. Roads were greatly improved; newly constructed canals provided the principal means of transportation. The perfection of Neilson's 'hot blast' furnace in 1828 gave potential industrialists an incentive to exploit the coal and iron resources of the Central Lowlands. The stage was now set for the greatest economic, social and environmental upheaval ever known in Scotland.

During the nineteenth century many parts of the Central Lowlands altered irrevocably in favour of intensive urban development. Where industry developed in an existing burgh, little regard was shown to incoming workers, many of whom had reluctantly come to the newly formed industrial areas simply to escape the hand-to-mouth existence forced on them by the break-up of the 'farmtoun' settlements and land enclosures. The rural poor of the countryside now formed the basis of an industrial poor in the urban areas of Scotland.

Glasgow gives one of the best examples of industrial urban development in Scotland during this period. From 1700 until 1775 the population of Glasgow expanded at a leisurely pace. The burgh was still contained within the medieval outline of the old town, which roughly followed the line of the High Street between the Cathedral and the River Clyde. During this time, new shipping links were established with America, trading was brisk, particularly in tobacco, and fortunes were made by a number of enterprising merchants, some of whom established themselves in newly constructed villa mansions in close proximity to the river. For the majority, however, including many reasonably wealthy citizens, the modest accommodation of the old town was more in accordance with their simple tastes. All lived in flatted property, gaining access by a dark, narrow turnpike stairway in much the same way as their counterparts in Edinburgh. A local historian could still record: 'Everyone is charmed by the appearance of Glasgow.' Another recorded, 'the free mixing of all groups within this Burgh'. Crime, it appears, was virtually unknown—perhaps this was wishful thinking. Many occupations, particularly those concerned with weaving and linen making, were still conducted in reasonable conditions, for the time, at home.

From 1780 to 1830, the population of Glasgow expanded rapidly from 40,000 to 200,000 people. A series of residential terraces was built in and around the area of George Square on land formerly owned by Hutchison's hospital to accommodate the burgh's wealthy citizens.

Further west again the lands of Blythswood were developed in a similar manner, and again for wealthy clients. Both developments followed a regular grid pattern, regardless of land configuration, which was in marked contrast to the meandering streets of the old town.

Speculation in land and property provides an interesting example in contemporary urban development in Scotland during this period. The landowner, or ground superior, could promote a development himself, but more commonly chose to feu the ground to a speculator, who in turn allocated plots to individual master masons to construct the actual houses. A set of plans was usually provided by the speculator's architect. These masons often employed fewer than twelve men, while many, having little working capital, were content to build one or two houses at a time, selling them as quickly as possible to obtain an early return on investment. The speculator required a steady nerve and an eye for sound, longterm investment in this highly uncertain field of business operation. The Lawrie brothers found this to their cost when they carefully laid out a substantial development beside the old village of Gorbals on the south side of the Clyde, only to find themselves surrounded by noxious industry and with little prospect of attracting a desired middle-class clientele. In the end, the properties were extensively divided up and rented out to near destitute incomers, who came in successive waves to seek employment in the burgh.

People fared little better in the old town, where scarcely a thought was given to the proper housing of the rapidly increasing work force. The existing houses facing the street had their roofs removed, one or two storeys were quickly added and many others were hurriedly constructed in the 'backlands'. Intensive exploitation of these areas created a pattern of squalor and deprivation which had scarcely any equal in Britain. The outcome of the situation is well described in *The History of Working-Class Housing*, edited by Stan D. Chapman:

> In the city centre by 1851 there was created an unhealthy crowded ghetto, with levels of population density varying from 500 to 1000 persons per acre. Provision for water supply, street cleansing, refuse and sewage disposal varied from the non existent to the primitive. Contaminated water, adulterated food, insecure employment, irregular wages were the lot of many; submersion in an over-supply of drink was the refuge of more than a few. Destitution, poverty, criminality, prostitution, child-beating, pawn-broking, drunkenness, shebeens, illicit distillation, all interrelated phenomena, flourished in so luxuriant a fashion that private individuals, voluntary associations and

municipal authorities, through conscience and necessity, had to intervene.

During the period from 1820 to 1840 there was a steady movement of people from the rural areas of Scotland and Ireland to the expanding industrial townships of the Central Lowlands. Potato blight in Ireland and in some parts of the Highlands during the mid-forties created widespread famine, and caused a rapid increase in the number of incomers to the industrial areas. This unhappy event coincided with the first large-scale development of heavy industries in central Scotland. While many of these unfortunate people were absorbed into the existing townships, others came in numbers to the new mining settlements beside the coal and iron deposits in North Lanark and North Ayrshire and Stirlingshire. Existing rural communities in these areas were quickly overrun by the rapid expansion of population. Short leases were imposed by local landowners on the mine owners which persuaded many of them to consider their operations on a strictly temporary basis. In spite of this, however, houses were often erected round the mines to a standard which might be considered reasonable for the period. Unfortunately, the number of miners required to work the mines was often greatly in excess of the number of houses provided for their families; this led to gross overcrowding, and extensive sub-letting by the occupants. Settlements formed in this way could hardly be described as communities; they were simply groups of people living at subsistence level in dreadful conditions with no traditional ties and little to give them a sense of identity or community. Effectively, single-class group settlements were being formed for the sake of economic expediency.

V

After 1840, a new type of tenement designed specifically to accommodate skilled working men and their families was erected in the industrial urban areas. These tenements were based on a three- or four-storey flatted block containing a variety of one- and two-room houses at each flat or 'landing'. Sanitary facilities were minimal; communal sinks were provided on the 'landing' or beside the stair tower; toilet accommodation was provided by a single privy at ground level.

This design was adopted as the basic housing unit for work people in the industrialised areas of central Scotland, undergoing countless local variations, improvements and refinements during the hectic building periods of 1867 to 1877 and 1893 to 1904. The design was a unique feature of Scottish housing. There were several reasons for this. Tightly packed, vertical housing units, divided into flats at each storey height, had been a common feature of Scottish townships from earliest times. The new tenement was simply part of a continuous process of development.

Under Scots law, the owner of a flat or house in a block of flats or tenements could enjoy full and separate ownership. This differed from current English practice in which a block of flats was invariably owned by one individual or an organisation. A block of flats or a tenement in Scotland could have a multiple ownership.

The sale of land in England was made by outright purchase of the freehold or by signing a lease which could be revised on expiry after an agreed period of time. In Scotland an outright purchase of land could also be made, but more commonly ground was feued by the owner to a prospective builder. The feu duty was a sum of money given in perpetuity to the ground superior by the holder of the title deeds. As a result of this, the initial cost of land for building was often more expensive in Scotland than in England, and legal costs were more onerous. Tradition and law, combined with current attitudes of the day, led speculators to build numbers of small one- and two-room units at high density on crowded urban sites. Gross overcrowding added to the congestion and often created intolerable living conditions in nearly new property.

The earliest government Act which was directly related to housing was concerned with danger to public health; the spread of disease from the poorest sections of the community was greatly feared. The threat was very real. Subsequent housing acts underlined the fears of the legislators, the majority of whom were all drawn from the wealthier classes in society. Nor had the possibility of revolution escaped the attention of the ruling group.

Housing reform now became an urgent necessity, but it was not until the 1860s that positive action was taken by Edinburgh and Glasgow City Councils to relieve intolerable conditions. Even then, efforts by the authorities appeared to be somewhat half-hearted and lacking initiative. A government Act of 1867 gave Edinburgh City Council powers to impose model by-laws for new housing, and to acquire and demolish condemned property, to erect new houses and to lease existing houses to evicted tenants. In practice, much of the rebuilding was left to private enterprise. A number of model tenements were erected, but these were hopelessly inadequate to deal with the housing requirements of those dispossessed by the demolitions.

In Glasgow the City Improvement Act of 1866 gave similar powers to the city council to demolish and rebuild some of the highly congested areas of old Glasgow. Loans of one and a quarter million pounds were authorised for the purpose. Incensed ratepayers objected to the imposition of an additional 6d (2½p) on the rates to service the loan. After initial enthusiasm, the project faltered; the commercial crisis of 1878 gave a pretext for further inaction. In 1888 work was resumed, largely due to the efforts of the City Health Officer, and by 1909 the Corporation had built over 2,000 houses in tenement blocks; it is significant and ironical that only a proportion of these were reserved for the poorest class of tenant.

Others tried to grapple with the problem of poor housing; a group called the Glasgow Workmen's Dwelling Company was established in 1890 to provide healthy and comfortable accommodation for working-class people. This organisation was able to construct some 200 houses before going into liquidation. These efforts, unfortunately, had little effect on the immense housing problem which now confronted the citizenry of Glasgow.

An entirely new approach to the provision of housing was also considered; credit societies were formed to enable working people to purchase their own homes; these societies were more successful in purchasing old houses than in building new properties, but several small ventures in new house construction took place in and around the Edinburgh district.

These projects foreshadowed the first experiment in co-operative house building in Scotland. The Edinburgh Co-op. Building Co. Ltd was formed in 1861. The rules of this organisation provided for a majority of building operatives among the ordinary directors. Influential support was given to the organisation to facilitate the purchase of land from sceptical or reluctant landowners. Several schemes were built in Edinburgh at Abbeyhill, Restalrig and Stockbridge; the design consisted of two-storey housing divided into upper and lower flats, with access to the upper flat on one side and access to the lower flat on the other. Individual gardens were provided, which was usual in this type of property. The company prospered, but lost its co-operative character when shares were offered for investment by the general public. By 1885 some 1,400 houses had been built by the company. People from Denmark showed considerable interest in the enterprise; the co-operative housing idea was adopted by Danish workmen in Copenhagen; it was also investigated by the Danish government, who eventually gave financial support to a number of workers' projects. From these humble beginnings, the co-operative housing movement spread throughout Scandinavia, and became a vital element in all house-building programmes in the Nordic countries during the twentieth century.

The proportion of housing built by these early co-operatives in Scotland was insignificant. Many of the groups, formed in a spirit of idealism, failed to prosper; the size and the complexity of the housing problem in Scotland was too great. It is clear also that the unusual combination of philanthropic endeavour and commercial enterprise must have been extremely difficult to sustain in face of the much favoured *laissez-faire* attitudes of the period. Both Liberal and Tory Governments of the day took little or no interest, nor were they prepared to render financial support, which is probably one of the main reasons for the unfortunate and premature demise of the co-operative housing movement in Scotland.

VI

As the century progressed, speculators continued to supply accommodation for renting to the majority of the population. Three-, four- and sometimes five-storey blocks surrounding communal 'greens' or courts became the dominant feature of the larger industrial townships in Scotland. These tenements now conformed to local authority building by-laws which sought to eliminate bad building practices and to introduce a form of local standardisation – the standard Glasgow tenement plan was entirely different from its more spacious counterpart in Edinburgh.

The Census of 1871 showed that over 70 per cent of the population lived in one or two rooms, and that most of this accommodation was in tenement property. Apparently, there was great demand for this type and size of accommodation. Contemporary social workers and local government officials maintained that the working classes were unwilling to spend a greater proportion of their income on rent to secure more spacious housing facilities. It was said that too much was spent on food, drink and clothing. People were also accused of being intemperate and lazy. Overcrowding was accentuated by the popular practice of taking lodgers into small households.

The occupants of the tenements had long been accustomed to minimal accommodation and to paying small rents for their former dwellings in rural areas or in the very old parts of the burghs. Living in one- or two-roomed houses was certainly based on traditional attitudes and current expectations of the period. It could also be said that the work force did not earn enough, consistently enough, to be able to command better accommodation. It was difficult for tradesmen to pay regular rents – for labourers it was impossible. The loss of a job during the recurring periods of industrial slump, or loss of earnings caused by ill health, meant near-destitution for many families. Lodgers were often taken in to augment meagre incomes and to act as a safeguard against hard times. In such trying circumstances, credit must be given to working people who attempted to live up to the middle-class standards of the period.

In 1890 the 'Housing of the Working Classes Act' was first introduced; this gave powers to local authorities to acquire land and to build houses for working-class people. Unfortunately, no money was provided by the exchequer and, as a result, houses built by local authorities under the Act were of a lower standard than those currently being erected by private enterprise. These developments were characterised by outside balcony access and shared toilet block on the back elevation.

VII

By 1900, 75 per cent of the population lived in an urban setting. In a short period of a hundred years the people of Scotland had virtually become a nation of town dwellers; many were now concentrated in the expanding industrial towns of the Central Lowlands. Practically everyone lived in rented accommodation. A rigid social stratification had also taken place amongst the population in the urban areas. A *laissez-faire* philosophy influenced almost all economic and social activity in Scotland; this was clearly manifested in the housing market. Most ventures in self help, or in co-operative housing, were either losing momentum or had ceased operations altogether. Speculation still provided the main driving force for most house-building activity. It is especially significant that many prominent social and temperance workers who served in the industrial areas, during this period, were openly opposed to any form of subsidy to provide decent housing for working people.

The period from 1893 to 1904 provided the last concerted period of house building in Scotland before the First World War. Fewer one- and two-apartment houses were constructed and several fine tenement developments were built to house persons enjoying stable occupations and reliable incomes. Parts of Marchmont and Bruntsfield in Edinburgh, Hyndland and Langside in Glasgow provide fine examples of this type of well-planned and spacious city layout. Unfortunately, these developments came too late to be of lasting value, and could not, in any case, be afforded by working people.

Several factors now combined to reduce the number of houses built by speculators in the first decade of the twentieth century: costs of feus, town rates, bank rate and legal costs all rose dramatically; a new taxation on sales of new houses was introduced by the government.

Speculators were also uncertain about the intentions, or the imagined intentions, of local authorities during this period; these bodies were now regarded as potential rivals in the housing market, and as such were not to be trusted. As a result, several potentially fine housing developments were never fully completed. By 1910, house building had virtually stopped in Scotland; a dramatic fall-off in the number of house completions was recorded, and with the advent of the First World War, house building ceased altogether.

An inflationary situation, created by wartime conditions, induced the government to bring in a form of rent control for all tenanted properties in 1915. This was the first attempt by any government to intervene decisively in the workings of the housing market in Scotland. Rising agitation by working people concerning housing conditions, particularly on the part of coal miners, finally led to the appointment of a Royal Commission on housing in 1912.

The report by the Commission was finally published in 1917. Here, for the first time, an official body recommended that the state should accept responsibility for housing the working classes and, further, that this responsibility should be backed up by financial assistance. According to the Commission, private enterprise had largely failed to provide adequate housing for lower-paid workers. The report stated that many lived in conditions which could only be described as terrible. 47.9 per cent of the Scottish population lived in one or two rooms, compared to only 7.1 per cent in England. Incredible densities of between 400 and 1,000 to the acre were recorded in Glasgow, Edinburgh and Dundee. Overcrowding standards in Scotland were set at three per room; the current English figure was two per room. Pronouncements were also made on the advantages and disadvantages of living in tenements, on the role of the speculative builder in housing and about the way in which ordinary people lived in Scotland.

Largely accepting the findings of the Commission, the government produced the House, Town Planning (Scotland) Act of 1919, often referred to as the 'Addison Act'. The legislation imposed on local authorities a specific duty to consider the housing needs of their district and to submit to the Scottish Board of Health proposals to build houses for the working classes. Generous financial help and advice on administrative problems were offered to all municipalities. Charges to the local rates were to be nominal; it was stated that the greater proportion of the building costs would be raised from central government funds.

VIII

The 1919 Act produced a total of some 25,500 houses over the three-year period from 1920 to 1923; the Commission had estimated that at least 250,000 new houses were required in Scotland. Admission of failure to produce an adequate supply of houses during this period was blamed on a number of factors. Obviously the local authorities were trying to cope with a new business situation and could not be expected to develop an expertise in this difficult field overnight; house-building costs had trebled since 1914 owing to a shortage of labour and materials; the building industry had gone into decline during the war and needed time to regroup and to reorganise in the immediate post-war period. In spite of these problems, however, some excellent local authority developments were carried out during this period. In Glasgow, under the 1920 Act, the Corporation built initially in the Riddrie and Craigton districts; the houses had stone-faced fronts and still embodied many excellent features of good-class stone tenements built before the war. These developments were followed by a substantial scheme at Moss Park which was based on layout plans designed for Letchworth Garden City in England. Adequate money was spent on landscaping and tree planting. Ironically, however, lower-paid workers could not afford to rent houses in this district; many were taken by skilled artisans and office workers. The population density in these districts was much lower than the comparable pre-war figure for newly constructed working-class housing in Glasgow; at Moss Park the density was under 50 persons to the acre. This compared very favourably with densities measured in hundreds around the older parts of the city.

Since provision of housing for renting had become the responsibility of central and local government, the pattern of house-building activities altered significantly; the speculative builder now played a subsidiary role in the building programme. Even the 1923 Housing Act, designed specifically to give speculators an incentive to build houses for lower-paid workers, failed to achieve the desired result. Speculators of the period, in common with their predecessors, were simply not interested in building for this unpopular and highly unreliable end of the housing market.

In 1924, the government turned once again to the local authorities to make provision for working-class housing. A new housing Act for 'general need' known as the 'Wheatly Act' allocated generous subsidies from central funds and recommended that substantial contributions should be taken from local rates. Rents were limited to enable lower-paid workers to take advantage of the new houses. The repayment period for capital expenditure incurred on housing built under the Act was to be extended from 20 to 40 years. Glasgow Corporation took advantage of the Act to build a substantial development at Knightswood on the western boundary of the city, and also a smaller development at Carntyne on the eastern perimeter of the city.

Unfortunately, not all local authorities were able to achieve the reasonable standard set by Glasgow in these areas. The Board of Health was compelled by the government of the day to reduce the costs of houses submitted to it for approval under the Act. Design standards were reduced to a minimum and builder-work specifications severely curtailed. The resultant product of these restrictions was a dreary rough-rendered brick box which was formless, practically shorn of all detail, colour or ornamentation and utterly lacking in imagination. This 'design' was reproduced by many local authorities with slight local variations and adaptations throughout Scotland until the beginning of the Second World War. The site layout plans were still based on English garden city plans, but now lacked continuity and were rendered utterly lifeless by minimal landscaping and the rigid and highly unimaginative application of local by-laws by municipal road engineers and burgh surveyors. Small burghs, burghs and cities all received a quota of these minimal-standard designs. Collectively, they marred the approaches to all urban areas and completely destroyed the continuity of domestic architectural design in Scotland.

In the latter half of the twenties and early thirties prices received for new housing fell steadily until 1932, when the Department of Health could report that building costs were roughly comparable with those currently available in 1914. Certainly the time for large-scale housing programmes and a general raising of standards seemed appropriate for Scotland. Unfortunately, a world economic crisis precipitated by the collapse of the New York Stock Market in 1929 obliged the British National Government to impose severe cuts on all social services which included the current housing programme. In 1932, the Wheatly subsidy was cut by a third, and by 1935 it was discontinued altogether. During the depression, it was argued that cuts were necessary due to the serious national economic situation. Fortuitously, there had also been a considerable reduction in builder-work prices since 1924. The government also decreed that local authorities should now concentrate on slum clearance work, and that all new housing for renting should be left to speculative builders. This was an idea which few house builders took seriously.

One redeeming feature of this unhappy period was the Housing Scot-

land Act of 1930, called the 'Greenwood Act', which gave encouragement to local authorities to clear slum properties in their districts. Relatively little in the way of slum clearance had been attempted since the
war in spite of the fact that a specific subsidy had been made available
to local authorities since 1923. This was due to an over-all shortage of
houses, which made the early demolition of existing sub-standard
property impracticable. The negotiation of these properties was difficult
and time-consuming, and not at all popular with local officials who were
responsible for the acquisition of such buildings.

Slum clearance schemes also created considerable problems for local
authorities in so far as many of the people who were thus displaced
came from the poorest sections of the community, containing a high
proportion of 'problem families' with low housekeeping standards. The
rents were of necessity lower than those charged for houses built under
the earlier housing Acts.

The Housing Scotland Act of 1935 augmented the 1930 Act by
giving a subsidy to allow local authorities to remove people from overcrowded property in places which did not necessarily come within slum
clearance areas. At that time it was estimated that overcrowding in Scotland was on average six times greater than in England. The level set for
overcrowding was low by contemporary standards; the living room could
still be used to sleep two persons, children under ten years were counted
as half-persons and babies were discounted altogether. The local authority
surveys which resulted from the Act had now exposed the immensity
of the overcrowding problem in Scotland. It was estimated that a quarter
of the working-class population still lived in overcrowded conditions, not
including persons living in sub-standard or slum property.

Under the 1930 and 1935 Acts, Glasgow Corporation built a number
of schemes throughout the city. Blackhill, Springfield Road and Carntyne South were amongst the largest of these developments. The houses
were built to a height of three storeys round communal 'back greens';
they were faced in a reconstituted stone which is a recognisable feature
of all slum clearance housing constructed in Glasgow during this period.
At Paisley, the largest slum clearance development in Scotland was constructed at Ferguslie Park, while Edinburgh Corporation built extensively
at Craigmillar, Niddrie and Pilton. Dundee and Aberdeen also built slum
clearance developments, while in Stirling the historic view to the north
and west from the Castle was marred by the construction of an ill-
considered scheme immediately below the lowest rocks of the ancient
fortification at Raploch.

In these areas provision for shopping and community services was hopelessly inadequate; little attention was given to the spaces between the buildings, landscaping was minimal or, more often, non-existent. It is difficult to believe that the promoters and the designers were genuinely concerned about these developments, or what happened to the people who occupied the houses. These minimal efforts appeared to be a simple product of administrative indifference, economic stringency, technological compliance and political expediency.

Little so far has been said about the activities of the private builders during the inter-war period in Scotland. It has already been noted that the role of the speculative builder was greatly reduced after the First World War. During the 1920s they showed little interest in building homes for general speculation or for renting to lower-paid workers. One company did in fact build a number of houses for renting at Cardonald in Glasgow and at Carrickvale in Edinburgh. These houses bore a remarkable similarity to those currently being erected by local authorities, and are now often mistaken for council housing developments of the same period.

It was not until the 1930s, however, that speculative builders began to take a real interest in the housing market – for the first time in fact since 1910. Encouraged by the government and assisted by a growing number of building societies who were prepared to lend money on small individual properties, private builders started to build two-storey and single-storey detached or semi-detached villas on peripheral burgh and city sites all over Scotland. A boom developed in houses built for sale between 1934 and 1939. This was the 'golden age' of the 'bijou' bungalow, ribbon development planning and suburban sprawl. The English home counties version of a Bangladesh bungalow had arrived in Scotland. Most burghs and cities attracted examples of this type of development, but perhaps the biggest and most striking were at Blackhall and Fairmilehead in Edinburgh, and Bearsden and Newton Mearns in Glasgow. The majority of private housing built during the inter-war period was constructed during this short period.

The outbreak of the Second World War brought all new proposals for local authority and private development to an end; the first twenty years of government intervention in the housing market and the application of state subsidy for housing were abruptly terminated.

It is particularly difficult to make an objective assessment of this period; prejudice is too well established, the failures are too obvious. A national housing problem had at least been officially recognised and a positive, if faltering, series of attempts had been made to find a solution. Local authorities had developed an expertise in the business of promoting and managing large- and small-scale housing developments. No one need doubt the difficulties faced by authorities in bearing the main responsibility for the promotion of the inter-war housing programme; it must have been obvious that the rehousing of some sections of the community would not be easy and would probably be unsuccessful. In the political, social and economic climate of the period, no one else was prepared to rehouse the poorest sections of the community.

In the private sector, builders had regained interest and re-entered the mass housing market during the late thirties, proving that they could serve demand when adequate financial backing was made available to prospective buyers. Many people were given an opportunity by way of a building society loan to become owner-occupiers for the first time in their lives. Unfortunately, this particular social revolution caused a complete break with traditional and regional forms of house building in Scotland.

Housing associations did very little work in Scotland during the inter-war period – they were simply not given the opportunity to show their capabilities or potential; little encouragement was given either by local authorities or by central government to these organisations. This is discussed in more detail later.

The task of providing new housing for the people of Scotland during this period was made infinitely more difficult by the alarming oscillations of party politics in Britain which bore heavily on housing policies, and by the highly questionable management of the economy by an 'amateur' styled treasury in Whitehall. These 'professional amateurs' persuaded the government to pursue policies more suited to the economic condition of the country at the turn of the century and, in so doing, made a mockery of attempts to provide an adequate, cohesive and continuous programme of housing improvement in Scotland. Unfortunately, similarly entrenched attitudes and postures affected their successors and their political 'masters' during the late forties, fifties and sixties, producing the same disastrous results in housing and in neighbourhood planning. The process, though now somewhat moderated, continues in the 1970s.

Tradition, social and cultural factors, resources and economic activity, political history, population, natural environment and climate have all conditioned the housing policies and programmes of the nation states in Europe. In Scotland, the sum total of these influences seems to have inhibited the growth of a successful housing policy for many years.

There are still, unfortunately, many aspects of Scottish housing which are unpleasant and give cause for concern. A recent Department of Environment report, the findings of which were mainly based on the 1971 Census figures, found that Scotland contains a very high proportion of the worst 5 per cent housing areas in Britain. Scotland enjoys a most unenviable reputation in this most important social field. It has been estimated that some 160,000 families live in accommodation which is below the 'official tolerable standard', while many more live in housing which meets the official standard and no more.

Scotland also enjoys the reputation of having some of the most inhuman, dreary and unimaginative post-war housing in the whole of Europe. The over-all standard of housing for working people is poor; environmental conditions exist in many Scottish housing areas which would simply not be tolerated in many European countries. Expectations and aspirations in housing are low; personal priorities in housing are often distorted by outdated concepts and attitudes. Scots accept appalling conditions in older housing with a terrifying stoicism, while the low standard of design and layout in many of the new housing developments excites little positive response or protest; a stupefying drabness exists in many Scottish housing developments which simply defies description. This prospect baffles and dismays sympathetic visitors from Europe, especially those concerned with housing and housing problems.

A more detailed comparison between Scotland and her European neighbours shows the following: 'in terms of space standards (measured in the number of average rooms per dwelling) a recent survey made by the EEC showed that Scotland with 3.8* is slightly ahead of France with 3.7 and Italy 3.5, but behind West Germany with 5.5, Netherlands 5.1 and England 4.6.

On the credit side, Scotland has an excellent record in the provision

*This figure was prepared by the Scottish Development Department.

of basic amenities such as WC, bath and piped water supplies in relation to her European neighbours who are all faced with the problem of coping with large rural populations. Both England and Holland also have a good record in this provision, but, surprisingly, over a third of the Dutch housing stock is still without flush sanitation.

Owner-occupation is rising throughout the EEC with England, Belgium and Italy clearly in the lead with 51 per cent, 55 per cent and 53 per cent respectively. The Italian figure requires some qualification owing to the fact that amenity standards in Italy are low in comparison with other European countries. France comes next with 43 per cent, while West Germany and Holland with 34 per cent and 36 per cent are only slightly ahead of Scotland which occupies bottom position with 31 per cent.

But perhaps the one most significant difference between housing in Europe and in Scotland is to be found in the choice of house type and range of housing tenure. Most countries in Europe can offer at least four distinct categories of tenure in new housing, while several can offer up to six categories. Total building programmes are also more evenly divided between tenure categories than in Scotland. The range of choice open to persons seeking a home in Scotland is more limited than anywhere else in Western Europe and, ironically, also in many parts of Eastern Europe. Choice in Scotland is restricted to two categories of new housing: public sector (which includes council housing, housing in the new towns and housing by the government body called the SSHA) and private sector.

Variety of tenure in Europe is largely due to the activities of groups known generally as housing associations or societies, which are run by a variety of independent 'non-profit'-making organisations mainly for the benefit of lower-paid workers. The groups vary enormously not only in size – which is related to organisation and territorial area – but also in the type of housing offered; they perform a valuable housing service in many countries and form a vital component in the development of national housing programmes throughout the Continent.

In Scotland, the housing co-operative movement hardly exists at all. In the period from 1950 to 1977, with the exception of two years, 1972 and 1976, completions by housing associations and housing societies have never exceeded two per cent of the total housing production in any given year. Successive British governments and Scottish local authorities in particular have given little support to housing co-operatives – and have only recently appreciated the value of housing associations – while the independent financial institutions, including many building societies, have been and still are suspicious, indifferent or even unaware of the investment potential offered by these groups.

Scotland, until very recently, built proportionally more public housing or state housing than any other country in Western Europe. During the four-year period from 1967 to 1970 housing construction in the public sector accounted for over 80 per cent of the total annual housing completions in Scotland. Even some of the socialist countries in Eastern Europe could not compete with this impressive figure.

Few countries in Western Europe rely to such an extent on the state or local authorities to promote housing programmes. According to the *Annual Bulletin of Housing Statistics* for 1976, state-promoted housing accounts for under 5 per cent of all completions in many countries; the notable exception was Austria, which recorded on that occasion state-housing completions of 7.3 per cent.

Significantly, in two East European countries, Czechoslovakia and Poland, state housing completions accounted for less than 25 per cent of the total production. In the same year the comparable figure in Hungary was 35 per cent, while Yugoslavia, Bulgaria and Romania built 40 per cent, 55 per cent and 57 per cent respectively.

Russia builds the biggest percentage of state-sponsored housing in Europe – 75 per cent, gives low priority to housing societies and reluctantly allows a certain amount of private building to take place in the outlying districts of the country. In many respects, current Russian housing programmes bear comparison with the Scottish housing programmes of the late sixties.

It appears that some priority is now being given to housing co-operative groups in Russia, and the number of houses built for the co-operatives is increasing annually. Recently, a Russian spokesman on housing suggested that all new housing construction in the urban areas should be based on the co-operative principle and argued that 'part-ownership' and participation in the administration of a housing co-operative encouraged social responsibility amongst the citizenry. Government spokesmen hasten to emphasise that the Soviet form of housing co-operative is based on group socialist principles as opposed to the profit-seeking principles of the 'pseudo-socialist' enterprises in Western Europe.

Most countries in Western Europe actively encourage owner-occupation, and few make as much distinction between the public and the private sector as in Scotland. Nothing could be more rigid and inflexible than the existing Scottish system of housing the population. In Germany, for example, a block of flats may contain families with a wide range of incomes and differently assessed subsidy allocations, while in

France a similar block often houses people holding differing forms of tenure – some flats are rented, rented under group ownership, or are in owner-occupation. Public sector housing in Scotland cannot allow for these differing forms of tenure and consequently allow for differing social groups to live in close proximity.

Following on from this is a brief description of housing policies and programmes in four European countries.

Belgium

Belgium is approximately one third the size of Scotland, has a population of 9.6 million, and is one of the most densely populated countries in Western Europe. The country is administered through centralised government departments from Brussels; there are nine provincial councils and over 2,500 local communes, some of which cover very small administrative areas.

The National Housing Institute of Belgium, founded in the mid-fifties, is a research and advisory body, which gives help to organisations concerned with housing and on a wide range of allied subjects. The work of the Institute is respected and appreciated; many of its recommendations have formed the basis for new housing legislation. It is responsible for the organisation of architectural competitions in Belgium and in the countries of the EEC, and also sponsors social and economic housing studies by students in Belgian universities. The Institute plays an important role as a central information centre on housing in Belgium and reports on current housing ideas and trends on radio and television at regular intervals.

The National Housing Society and the National Rural Property Society play vital roles in the implementation of social housing policies and programmes in Belgium. These societies are semi-state bodies and are administered by a board of directors; government departments directly concerned with social housing programmes are represented on the board. The two groups prepare housing programmes, administer and give technical advice to locally based associated housing societies charged with the task of carrying out housing development and construction. There are at least 300 local societies associated with the National Housing Society and over 50 with the Rural Property Society. These local societies are partly financed by the national organisations and partly from funds granted by the local commune in which they operate. The societies buy land – often from the local commune, engage local architects to prepare house plans, act as client and promoter during the construction period, and are responsible for renting, management and maintenance of completed housing developments. Depending on local conditions and requirements, they may sell new houses. The local rural societies, however, only build houses for sale. The national organisations are responsible for approving local land purchase and housing development plans and are generally responsible for ensuring that quality and value for money are obtained. The societies have been responsible for producing some of the best and most imaginative housing in Belgium.

Owner-occupation is actively and positively encouraged by the government; over 55 per cent of the housing in Belgium is owner-occupied. Government-sponsored mortgages are available for the purchase of social housing from the national societies. The government will also grant an additional mortgage to supplement a commercial mortgage, which is usually in the order of 60-70 per cent. Tax concessions and reductions in legal fees are also granted to owner-occupiers.

People from all income groups are encouraged to build their own houses by a high level of financial assistance granted to individual house-building projects. This is in direct contrast to Scotland where few people expect to build their own homes. The individual approach is a marked feature of house building in Belgium, particularly in the country districts. After the Second World War, workers in the mining industry were encouraged by the government to borrow money for house purchase at low rates of interest from the Belgian National Savings Bank – an unimaginable situation in Scotland even in the 1970s.

The first post-war housing Act, which was passed in 1948, also encouraged owner-occupation by giving state backing to borrowers from the National Savings Bank, and other officially approved credit sources. The Act forms the basis of the current state housing subsidy system and allows substantial sums of money to be allocated for the building and purchase of 'social dwellings' in Belgium.

In 1949, another Act granted financial support to two national housing societies, while the government took responsibility for the costs of public services and roads and for setting out public open spaces within housing development areas sponsored by the housing societies. A National Housing Account was also established to finance national social housing policies. In 1953, the government created a further Act, which encouraged the demolition of slum property by granting a sum of money equal to the market value for any property demolished by local communes.

From 1956 to 1974 the period is dominated by the housing Acts of 1956 and 1967. An extract from an official programme is reproduced below:

Summary of the Main Stipulations of the 1956 Act:

(a) A National Housing Institute was established which would be commissioned with the drawing up of a permanent inventory of the housing needs, the investigation of the possibilities to meet these needs and with other research work. The Institute delivers advice on all kinds of housing problems and is allowed to build experimental dwellings. The activity of the study and research service of the National Society was stopped.

(b) The General Savings Bank and Pension Fund was authorised to finance the furnishing of the social dwellings.

(c) The terminology 'National Society for Low-cost Houses and Apartments' and 'low-cost dwellings' was replaced by 'National Housing Society' and 'social dwellings'.

(d) The activity of the National Housing Society was considerably extended. Thus the National Society itself was thenceforth allowed to build houses and to lend money to private persons for the building and necessary furnishing of social dwellings.

(e) The state premium system was extended until December 31, 1960 (given permanent character in 1964).

(f) Likewise the term of the 1949 Act was extended until December 31, 1960 and it was stipulated that the National Society would dispose of the necessary capital for an annual investment of 2,4 milliard BF for each of the years from 1956 up to and including 1960 (given permanent character in 1964).

(g) The Board of Directors of the National Society was renewed and replaced by a council consisting of a president and ten directors who are all nominated by the King.

By the ministerial decree of June 30, 1956 which was promulgated in enforcement of the Act of March 16, 1954 concerning the control on certain institutions for public welfare, two revisers were appointed at the National Housing Society.

The Act of March 16, 1954 has repeatedly been modified and

completed. Thus the royal decree no. 4 of April 18, 1967 introduced some general strengthening enactments concerning the exercise of the control on the institutions for public welfare summed up in the above-mentioned Act. The royal decree no. 88 of November 11, 1967 transferred the National Housing Society from category C to category B of the institutions for public welfare.

In addition at each approved building society a commissioner was appointed exercising a supervision similar to the one exercised by the governmental commissioners referred to in the Act of March 16, 1954.

On July 3, 1967 an Act was promulgated by which the government was authorised to enlarge the activity of the National Housing Society and the National Landed Property Society — The National Landed Property Society is a state-controlled institute dealing with rural development, social housing and land consolidation. This Act caused no changes in the traditional activity of the National Society and its approved building societies. Its aim was to authorise the National Society to build dwellings itself of which by priority the personnel of new or expanding industries would take possession, regardless of their income.

By the royal decree of December 10, 1970 all the valid enactments concerning modest dwellings and small landed properties, the involved public institutions, the state allowances for social housing and slum clearance, were co-ordinated into one code, called the Housing Code. This code was ratified by the Act of July 2, 1971. By this Act all the previous separate Acts, except for a few provisions, were abolished so that thenceforward only the co-ordinated text has been legally valid.

From January 1, 1956 to December 31, 1974 a total of 140,594 dwellings were put out to tender, 17,788 of which were built in accordance with the system 'purchase-sale promise'. During this same period the number of houses sold amounted to 40,373.

Netherlands

The Netherlands is approximately one third the size of Scotland, has a population of 13 million and is the most densely populated country in Western Europe. The principal promoters of housing in the Netherlands are housing associations, the municipalities, institutional investors and private builders.

Housing associations serve the community by building houses to high standards both in terms of design and in quality. They are responsible for constructing some of the best housing designs in the Netherlands. House building by these associations is largely financed by the government, which means that they can participate in the national housing effort without having to amass capital; they have no shareholders and are considered to be non-profit-making organisations. There are about 1,000 institutions (1972) in the Netherlands, approved under the Housing Act, which are eligible for government finance and for a subsidy towards the housing management. These institutions now cover about 80 per cent of the local municipalities and have greatly extended their sphere of influence, especially during the last ten years. This is due not only to increased activity on the part of the associations themselves, but also because the municipal authorities have been compelled by law to leave their own building activities to these groups. Many municipalities are also transferring housing property to the associations. These associations vary greatly in size from small groups who are responsible for sponsoring and managing up to 50 dwellings, to those who manage over 10,000 dwellings. The largest associations usually operate in the urban regions and the small associations in rural municipalities. Currently they account for approximately 36 per cent of the total annual housing completions in the Netherlands.

In principle, the Netherlands legislature does not believe that the municipal authorities should build and manage housing development. Municipalities are expected to confine themselves to regulating and supporting other groups in this field. In practice, however, this does not always happen, and certainly did not happen in the past. In a number of municipalities no housing association exists; in others associations are often available, but they are incapable of sponsoring large development plans. Under these circumstances, municipalities are permitted to sponsor house-building programmes. The central authorities, however, believe that the management of the completed housing should be placed in the hands of a housing association as soon as possible. In recent years, there has been a general decrease in municipal house-building activity; this is due to official government policy.

The institutional investors, constituting the third-largest group of housing promoters in the Netherlands, are pension funds, insurance companies, savings banks and investment companies. Continuity of house-building activity on the part of these investors is considered to be of great importance for the national housing production. As might be expected, these investors expect to make a profit and as a direct result of this the interest rate of the government loans for Housing-Act dwellings is constantly adjusted to the interest rate on the capital market. This principle is also applied to land costs for both groups. Apart from acting as an important promoter of house building, the institutions lend money to people who build dwellings for owner-occupation, to certain of the housing associations and to institutions for housing the elderly.

The promotion of private home ownership is encouraged by the central authorities in the Netherlands. Compared with many other countries in Western Europe, private home ownership is proportionally small – 36 per cent of the population own their own homes. In spite of this, promoters of privately owned dwellings form the second-largest group of house builders in the country.

Owing to rapidly rising building costs, private house ownership now threatens to move beyond the reach of many lower-income groups. A new scheme was introduced in 1971 to promote private house ownership for financially less well-off people, to augment the existing facilities for the purchase of new, privately owned dwellings (municipal guarantee with government participation for interest and repayments, as well as annual grants towards the running costs). Persons having an income below a certain limit can be granted an interest-free loan to enable them to buy a new dwelling. Unfortunately, substantial interest was shown in the venture and consideration of new applications had to be temporarily suspended. Stringent planning requirements compel housing promoters to conform to local development plans; this has restricted the worst excesses of private developers and builders in the private sector.

Local municipalities have been able to purchase large plots of land for house-building purposes; this has most certainly influenced the cost of land in the Netherlands. Compulsory purchase of land for housing is based on fair compensation and seems to be generally favoured by the public. This greatly helps to avoid delays, assists conveyancing and reduces costs for municipal land purchase. There appears to be a reasonable degree of collective social responsibility on the part of the population in the Netherlands; this is fortunate in a crowded country where land is at a premium.

The following is an extract from an official information sheet showing a proposed house-building programme for the Netherlands:

House Building Programme 1975

1. 48,300 rented dwellings (35.6 per cent of the total programme) to be built by housing associations and municipalities.

   Financing. 44,000 dwellings of housing associations and municipalities to be financed with loans granted to the municipalities by the central government. (The municipalities furnish the loans in equal amounts to the housing associations.) The rate of interest of the loans is 9 per cent per year; interest and redemption are paid on an annuity basis. A limited number can be built for owner-occupancy with special assistance from the housing associations.

   4,300 dwellings, exclusively to be built by housing associations and financed with loans to an amount of 90 per cent of the over-all building costs, which the associations can obtain on the capital market with a guarantee from the municipality. The housing associations must furnish the remaining 10 per cent of the over-all building costs from own funds.

   Subsidies. An annual sum paid to the municipalities by the central government (the municipalities furnish an annual grant in the same amount to the housing associations). The annual grants are broken down in about 10 years as a result of rent increases.

2. 31,250 rented dwellings to be built by private enterprise (23.0 per cent) (including institutional investors).

   Financing. With own funds or by means of loans obtained on the capital market in the form of a mortgage.

   Subsidies. As above, except that the central government pays the annual grants to the entrepreneur direct.

3. 31,250 owner-occupied dwellings (23.0 per cent) (private ownership).

   Financing. The owners must arrange for financing themselves. If in order to finance part of the over-all building costs of the dwelling – as a rule up to at most 95 per cent of these costs – the owner obtains a loan, the municipality can guarantee the interest and redemption of the loan. The central government can take for its account 50 per cent of any loss the municipality might sustain as a result of the afore-mentioned guarantee.

Subsidies. An annual grant, which the central government pays to the owner of the new dwelling direct. Each year this grant is reduced by one tenth of the original sum paid.

4. 24,500 rented and owner-occupied dwellings (18 per cent) to be built without a government subsidy (free sector dwellings).

Financing. The owners of the free sector dwellings will have to finance the building of these dwellings themselves. The financing of the owner-occupied dwellings can be guaranteed by the municipality for dwellings which are not too expensive. If the over-all building cost of such a dwelling does not exceed a given limit, the central government can take for its account 50 per cent of any loss the municipality might sustain as a result of the guarantee given.

West Germany

West Germany is slightly larger than Britain in terms of land area, has a population of 61.5 million and is divided into eleven federal states or Länder, which act as the administrative regions for the country. There are reputedly as many dwellings as families in Germany. Many of these properties have been constructed during the last 25 years, are in reasonable condition, located in appropriate areas, and offer the most generous floor area per person in the whole of Europe. Standards in quality, finish and landscaping are high by comparison with other European countries and are certainly much higher than in Scotland.

Neither the state, nor the federal states, promote or build houses, while local authorities are responsible for only a very small percentage of housing promotions; these are built mainly to house local authority employees. Most new housing in Germany is built by private builders, or by independent housing associations. This does not mean that these groups are financed entirely from private funds. In 1971, for example, 50 per cent of all housing completions by private builders were partially or wholly subsidised by the government. It should also be noted that housing associations in Germany also build non-subsidised housing for private organisations.

Direct government loans covering up to 40-50 per cent of land and construction costs are available to house builders carrying out social housing programmes, with the interest being made payable during the early years of the loan. In addition, housing associations and housing companies are able to get private loans from banks and insurance companies for up to 40 per cent of total building costs at liberal rates of interest. Tax deductions are available to housing associations, to companies and to private individuals, and rent rebates may be claimed by people with low incomes for rented property.

West Berlin is a special case in point; here, 90 per cent of all housing built or rebuilt since the war has been promoted by housing associations. The West Berlin authorities have commissioned some 14 non-profit organisations to take part in a series of urban renewal programmes. To encourage promotion of housing in Berlin, government loans are given to housing associations to cover 65 per cent of costs for 100 years at 0.5 per cent interest. Areas designated for redevelopment are cleared only when reconstruction is assured, and people displaced from these areas have their removal expenses paid or are rehoused locally, wherever possible.

The German Federal Government supports the basic principle of owner-occupancy, believing that it gives a citizen a feeling of responsibility, makes him more self-reliant and encourages him to exercise his own initiative.

The First Housing Act 1950 provided for three different forms of housing finance:

1. 'Social' housing subsidised directly out of public funds. It was this class only which benefited from direct state subsidies. The primary aim of these schemes was to provide reasonable accommodation for persons with limited incomes.
2. Housing assisted by tax concessions. The assistance given in this case was only indirect and took the form of concessions in respect of income tax and the local tax on land and buildings.
3. Privately financed housing. Apart from being allowed to claim a higher depreciation allowance for income tax purposes, owners of such property received no public support, direct or indirect; on the other hand there were no restrictions as to the persons to whom the property could be let, or as to the rents which might be charged.

The Second Housing Act 1956 established that priority should be given to persons who wanted to invest their savings, especially in the form of a 'family home'. This prescribed that the building of family homes should, as a matter of principle, be given priority over all other forms of building. The sponsors of the Second Housing Act also believed that a wider distribution of private property would be achieved by encouraging owner-occupation by persons from lower-income groups and would, in the words of an official government publication, 'create a freer social order'.

The government social housing programme is carried out through the agencies of non-profit housing associations and limited dividend housing companies. After the war these groups, which included trade unions, church organisations and industrial and financial corporations, were set up with government backing to provide housing for lower- and medium-income families at reasonable terms. Over 2,000 of these groups now operate through West Germany, building a variety of flats and houses, and in some cases are responsible for the creation of whole district areas. The projects are situated mainly in the industrial and urban areas of the country. Currently, they account for 40 per cent of all new housing completions in Germany.

One of the best-known housing associations in Germany is the trade union-sponsored group called Neue Heimat (New Housing), which was formed in 1926 by the General German Union as a limited non-profit organisation to build houses for renting in Hamburg. After the Second World War the organisation took over the assets and responsibilities of the pre-war group, linked up with other union groups and gradually extended its field of operations throughout Germany.

Initially, Neue Heimat received financial backing from the German trade unions. An early decision was made to obtain additional capital from private sources at competitive rates of interest and to investigate new forms of housing finance within the existing capital market. Resulting from this, a close liaison was formed between the German mortgage institutions and Neue Heimat, which enabled it greatly to expand its activities in the low-cost housing market. In addition, the organisation took advantage of an income tax law which allowed industrial employers to grant mortgage loans to employees from taxable income. A considerable number of houses were built for low-income families using this method of housing finance.

Throughout the 1950s, Neue Heimat acted as a powerful pressure group by urging the German government to provide funds for social housing programmes in Germany. The organisation took the initiative in this matter by suggesting (to the government) methods of overcoming the current housing shortage. It was of course prepared to back this up by practical action—which is something the British trade union movement has never considered necessary or desirable.

Neue Heimat called for a general programme of housing for lower-income groups and for a national assessment of local needs and priorities. Federal districts and local communities were to be directed to make land available at a fair price by using legal procedures to stop speculative practices. Where possible, housing in the urban areas was to be built in the form of garden estates. The provision of schools, hospitals, community centres, kindergartens and churches were to be the subject of a special programme. The creation of segregated housing for special-income or professional groups was to be avoided. Non-profit housing co-operatives were to be given priority in all local housing programmes.

In 1961, Neue Heimat extended the field of its operations from housing to cover a programme of urban renewal. At this time, a shortage of government capital had made comprehensive development in the urban areas very difficult. The unions believed that adequate provision had to be made for ancillary services in urban housing developments. To meet this requirement Neue Heimat formed an alliance with a private industrial company to provide shopping facilities in new housing development areas. It also founded a research organisation to investigate problems concerned with area planning (market research), regional development and the reconstruction of cities.

In 1963, Neue Heimat assumed a major role in regional and urban reconstruction on behalf of the German unions. A non-profit organisation, Neue Heimat Kommunal, was formed to build social buildings such as community centres, schools, kindergartens, libraries and hospitals.

In 1969, the German unions endorsed their support for planned regional development and urban reconstruction; they authorised Neue Heimat to augment its activities by assisting the organisation to form a large subsidiary company, Neue Heimat: Staedtbau. This group was formed to construct industrial buildings for a variety of clients.

Neue Heimat is headed by an executive board of six members whose terms of reference are still controlled by the German unions. The policies of the organisation are agreed by boards of supervisory councillors from the unions and passed to the management for executive action. Current policies include a maximum of 4 per cent return on all investment by the unions and an agreement to accept paid-up basic capital only in the event of dissolution. Housing is to be built for renting or for selling to a wide section of the population within a regulated costing programme. Neue Heimat works closely with other union-based business groups; these include a union bank, insurance and property insurance companies and the consumer co-operative groups.

Neue Heimat believes that it has made an important contribution to planning, urban design and architecture in Germany. It provides approximately a sixth of all social housing construction in the country, sets competitive standards in terms of price and quality and offers a complete range of technical, financial, administrative and managerial services to many sections within the community. Currently, it is attempting to sponsor long-term building programmes with the specific intention of stabilising the cyclical nature of the building industry in Germany.

France

France is approximately two and a half times the size of Britain, has a population of 51 million as opposed to 55 million and supports one of the most centralised government administrations in Western Europe.

The country is divided up into 21 regions, each of which is responsible for carrying out national planning and building regulations in much the same way as local authorities do in Scotland. House building in France can be roughly divided into the public and private sectors. Financial assistance is given by the government to all social housing projects in the public sector and to roughly two thirds of housing built for the private sector. Housing construction in the public sector is dominated by an organisation called Habitations à Loyer Modéré (HLM) the origins of which go back to the last century; it was conceived as a private organisation with a charitable background which aimed to improve living conditions for workers in the industrial areas of France.

The French government increasingly relies on this organisation to provide housing for many social groups in France. In 1971, the HLM accounted for roughly 30 per cent of all French housing completions. With financial assistance from the central authority, HLM has broadened its housing programme to cover moderate-income groups without relaxing its traditional emphasis on building homes for the lowest-income groups in French society. Special programmes have been instituted to help young married couples with moderate incomes and for old people and students. The HLM is divided into three sections: public offices, mortgage companies and housing co-operatives. The character of the public office section was altered in 1971. In an attempt to increase efficiency and to reduce administrative difficulties, the public offices were reconstituted as quasi-commercial organisations; these groups build houses for rent and for sale to low-income groups, and also act as planners and co-ordinators for local housing programmes. The public offices account for approximately 44 per cent of the total HLM building programme.

The mortgage company section is divided into two groups. The first was created under government auspices by public savings banks, family allowance organisations and works groups set up by employers to house employees and to build houses for rental under the same conditions as the public offices section. The second group primarily assists people to buy a house or flat in a development constructed by a building company associated with HLM. Recently, these HLM mortgage groups were authorised to initiate house-building programmes themselves. The mortgage section accounts for approximately 40 per cent of the total HLM building programme.

The housing co-operative section of HLM builds homes for rental and 'delayed' sale. In the case of a 'delayed' sale a co-operative offers a house or flat initially as a rented property; after paying the cost of the dwelling over a period of 20-25 years, the tenant is able, if he wishes, to become a house owner. Persons renting houses from a co-operative group make an initial deposit of 10 per cent of original cost which entitles them to a permanent home within a co-operative development. This section accounts for approximately 16 per cent of the total annual HLM building programme.

Government ministries are empowered to direct the affairs of the HLM in administrative, financial and technical matters; they are responsible for checking housing standards, floor areas and maximum costs. In 1970, housing costs, which were traditionally based on a square metre measurement, were altered in favour of a cost based on the nummer of bedrooms per house; this is intended to give more flexibility to house builders. The government provides most of the finance both directly and indirectly for the house-building operations of the HLM. The organisation is also granted special tax allowances and is relieved from paying corporation tax, value added tax and licence duties.

In France, dwelling subsidies are graded according to the standards of the dwelling, and cover dwellings both for sale and for rent. Further, generous family allowances, which are related to income (centrally and not locally assessed), enable all to choose between rental and ownership. This system produces mixed tenure and quite a considerable degree of social integration, which is impossible to achieve under present conditions in Scotland. In this respect, the activities of the HLM particularly serve to blur the private and public sectors in new housing development in France.

3 HOUSING IN SCANDINAVIA

I

The Scandinavian countries have developed remarkably high living
standards, despite a lack of natural resources, small populations, uncompromising terrains and unrewarding climates. The standard of living
in any one of the four Nordic states is much higher than the comparable
standard in Scotland. More specifically, the quality of housing in Scandinavia is amongst the best, if not the best, in Europe; Scotland, on the
other hand, rates very badly in this respect, containing, as already noted,
some of the poorest housing in the whole of the European continent.

A discerning visitor from this country cannot fail to appreciate the
striking contrast between housing achievements in Scandinavia and those
in Scotland. The standard of housing design, in quality, detail and finish,
in contrast and variety, is of a very high order. These levels of excellence
are also maintained in the layout of many post-war residential areas; in
these developments the relationship of one house to its neighbour and
the careful organisation of spaces between the buildings immediately
create a sense of belonging and a feeling of community. Schools, shops
and community services, including nursery schools, baby-minding
centres, mother-care centres, premises for young people, libraries and
amateur theatres, are planned simultaneously to complement the
housing areas. Many of these facilities are often completed before the
first occupants take up residence in a new area — an idea which is in-
conceivable in Scotland. Clearly, the important concept of community
planning has been appreciated by politicians at national and local level,
by promoters and not least by planners and architects.

The people of Scandinavia are obviously concerned about the
physical background to their lives; they are more involved and interested
in domestic planning and design problems than their counterparts in
Scotland. It is not uncommon for prospective occupants to be consulted
during the early planning period of a neighbourhood area, to be asked
for opinions on the grouping of houses, and to examine house plans.

There is also a degree of social integration amongst the working population in Scandinavia which is impossible to contemplate in Scotland. A
labourer and a professional man in Scandinavia may not share the same
interests, ideals or cultural values, but at least they can and do occupy houses
in the same block of flats and also send their children to be educated at a

local school without feeling in any way different or out of step with the rest of the community.

Existing housing areas are not shattered and spattered by mindless vandalism which characterises housing layouts in some parts of Scotland; miraculously, glass stays in telephone boxes and bus shelters, trees are not hacked or uprooted, grass and plants are not trodden into the ground by mindless boots.

A sense of bewilderment is often experienced by visitors when faced with the reality of the Nordic domestic scene—how was it done?—how was it achieved? Allowing for many imperfections, why is housing in Scandinavia so much better than housing in Scotland?

In many respects Scandinavians are not greatly dissimilar either in character or in background to many people in Scotland. The populations of the Scandinavian countries and of Scotland are not vastly different in size: Sweden with some 8 million tops the list, Denmark comes next with 5 million, Norway and Finland have 3.9 million and 4.7 million respectively. Scotland has some 5.5 million people to support. Norway, Sweden, Finland and Scotland contain vast areas of wild, desolate and uncompromising terrain surrounded by rugged and extended coastlines. The vagaries of a northerly, maritime climate make the harvesting of arable crops in Scotland and Norway a hazardous business; in all countries the winters are long and the days are shorter and darker than anywhere else in Europe. Scotland has more agricultural land than Norway and is marginally better off in terms of natural resources. Scandinavia suffers from a lack of natural resources; the Nordic countries have to rely on the genius and expertise of their people to produce a state of economic well-being; they are committed to ambitious exporting programmes to maintain present high living standards. Scotland, by virtue of her complicated economic ties with England, now the third most densely populated country in the world, must export to survive at all.

All countries are engaged to some degree in fishing, while forestry is important in Norway, Sweden and Finland, and potentially so in Scotland. Scotland and Norway support large merchant fleets; Scotland, Sweden and Denmark all build ships and have developed considerable skills in many aspects of engineering. An abundance of swift-flowing rivers and sizeable lakes has given rise to the production of hydro-electric power in Norway, Sweden, Finland and Scotland.

Finally, all countries enjoy a rich cultural heritage; this still applies to Scotland despite serious neglect and denegation by many Scots during the nineteenth and twentieth centuries.

Here, unfortunately, the similarities between Scotland and her Nordic neighbours end. Several important factors separate and differentiate Scotland from these countries. The first of these is concerned with the timing and the volume of industrial development in Scandinavia and in Scotland; the second follows on from the first in that Scandinavians managed to maintain and to adapt cultural and traditional links with the past during the period of industrialisation at the beginning of the twentieth century. The third and last factor, and easily the most contentious, is concerned with national priorities in the respective countries.

Fortunately for all Scandinavians, industrial development was delayed until the beginning of the twentieth century and, even when development did take place, it was less concentrated and less destructive than the earlier and cruder developments which occurred in Scotland. Rapid movements of populations from rural to urban situations did not occur in Scandinavia until the 1930s. By this time, both government and local authorities were in a position to deal effectively and humanely with the difficult problem of population movement on a substantial scale. The Scandinavian landscape was not torn up, piled up and made hideous by indiscriminate mining operations, nor was it strewn with the concentrated accretions of heavy industrial developments. Scandinavians also mercifully escaped the worst excesses of the nineteenth-century Scottish factory towns.

The economic depression of the late 1920s and early 1930s created much hardship for Scandinavians, but these deprivations did not appear to stultify their attitudes or their aspirations. Unlike Scotland, they were able to carry out a programme of social and economic improvement in housing during the post-depression and post-war periods which was to become the envy of Europe.

Cultural and traditional links with the past were not shattered in Scandinavia during the period of industrial development. Somehow, many crafts were adapted and turned to advantage by industrial processes instead of being destroyed or cheapened by them. Somehow, an intuitive sense of good design — a characteristic of many non-industrialised peoples throughout the world — was preserved and translated into a range of increasingly sophisticated and beautiful products: items of pottery, glass, textiles and furniture from Scandinavia soon gained recognition in the international trading markets of the world.

In housing, few traditions and features of the past were incorporated into designs; new ideas and techniques had to be developed and assimilated to meet changing conditions and a general raising of living standards. Quality and value for money were emphasised; cheap or expedient solutions to housing problems were regarded as a poor investment by the vast majority of the population.

Before the industrial revolution, Scandinavians lived in small communities isolated by long distances and rough terrain and were at the mercy of a hostile climate; this helped to foster a spirit of initiative and independence in which the value of a collective effort was quickly recognised and understood. They were accustomed to types of work which required periods of individual and collective effort at different times of the year. This life style seems to engender a sense of social responsibility and encourages self-participation in the running of communal affairs. Fortunately, these admirable characteristics have been generally observed by the promoters, officials and designers of the new urban settlements. There is continual discussion about the nature, functions and effectiveness of agencies and institutions involved in the promotion and management of housing, more widespread and informed public discussion on the subject and far less passive acquiescence of squalor and cheap solutions to housing problems. People expect to be involved, to be considered and to have an effective say in where and how they live.

The third and most controversial difference between the Nordic states and Scotland is concerned with national priorities. Housing is given a much higher national priority in Scandinavia than in Scotland. The proportion of the gross national product spent on housing in the respective countries, using the figures for 1975, is as follows: Sweden 4.2; Denmark 4.6; Norway 5.5; Finland 7.0; Britain 3.9.

Britain (Scotland) is much more concerned about national and international status than the Scandinavian countries; this unhealthy obsession is an expensive luxury which Scotland does not need and simply cannot afford. There is apparently a compulsive need to spend public money on a variety of status-seeking enterprises and endeavours to the continuing detriment of all essential community services in Britain.

The Scandinavian countries, in common with many nations, incur trade deficits with other trading nations throughout the world; during a period of heavy deficit, Scandinavian governments have always considered a reduction in housing expenditure to be a last resort. Britain (Scotland) has incurred numerous trade deficits since the end of the Second World War; in times of crisis—these usually occur regularly every 2-4 years—the government inevitably cuts back spending on housing and other vital community services. A rising rate of unemployment is regarded as another regrettable, but necessary, solution to recurring economic problems in Britain. This insidious activity obviously has an adverse effect on housing programmes, and also reflects on people's ability to pay for better housing, or indeed to pay for reasonable accommodation at all.

The governments in the Scandinavian countries have never shown such blatant and cynical disregard for the welfare of their peoples; they have developed a remarkably sane approach to the management of financial, political, technological and economic affairs. Scandinavians are fortunate in that they could not afford to emulate the status-seeking excesses of successive British governments even if they were so inclined; the size of populations and the availability of economic resources safeguard and ensure a reasonable approach to most national policies and programmes in Scandinavia.

II

Before describing some of the more outstanding characteristics of individual housing programmes in the Nordic countries, some of the main differences between housing in Scotland and Scandinavia should be appreciated. It has already been mentioned that ordinary people in Scandinavia are considerably more interested and involved in housing and in housing programmes and that this has been a vital factor in the creation of viable and successful communities in these countries.

National governments and local municipalities do not concern themselves directly with housing promotion, construction, management or maintenance, except in special circumstances. There is a range of organisations in each country which promote, construct and manage housing in Scandinavia and which are largely unknown in Scotland. Particular attention is drawn to the contribution made by mutual building co-operatives and associations to house-building programmes. These organisations are responsible for building substantial neighbourhood areas, for helping to keep housing costs to reasonable levels and for promoting a great deal of research and development in the building industry. They are the creators of standards and the prime movers of many housing programmes in Scandinavia. The trade unions also take an active and positive part: they were responsible for the creation of the early mutual societies in these countries. One of the largest and most influential of the societies is the Svenska Rikbyggen of Sweden which is described in more detail later in this chapter.

National house-building programmes in Scandinavia cover a much wider section of the population than in Scotland. A quotation from the introduction to an official publication—*Housing in the Nordic Countries*—underlines the thought behind the development of housing projects:

No special provision is made for working-class families. The social

structure of new housing areas is about the same as that of the population as a whole. This does not imply that all class distinction has
been abolished, but indicates that the traditional division of the
population in working-, middle- and upper-class groups no longer
characterises that part of the housing stock which was produced after
the war.

The national governments of the Scandinavian countries give considerable financial support to house-building programmes. It has long been
accepted that housing subsidies are necessary and desirable to house the
families of lower-paid workers. The methods of payment, if somewhat
cumbersome, are fairer to all sections of the community than those
which are presently applied in Scotland. One great social advantage
gained from the subsidy system is that people of differing means are
able to live in close proximity to each other. The deliberate creation of
housing areas for lowest-paid workers has never been popular, nor considered socially desirable in Scandinavia.

Scandinavians have always been concerned about obtaining maximum
value for money in housing. In Scotland, housing officials are obsessively
concerned about the initial capital costs of housing. Housing expenditure
for maintenance, it appears, is another problem — another budget! In
Scandinavia total costs of construction, maintenance and management
are carefully considered and included in all repayment calculations. The
quality of materials and of finish becomes important when maintenance
and management payments have to be taken into consideration in the
over-all costing of housing projects.

Official support is also granted to promoters and constructors of
housing in Scandinavia. In addition to assistance from governments,
numerous other organisations allocate funds to finance house-building
programmes. Some of these organisations are described later in this
chapter.

People are prepared to pay more for housing in Scandinavia than in
Scotland. A well-designed house set in a carefully planned neighbourhood area is valued and appreciated. It is also accepted by most Scandinavians that a mixed economy cannot support excessively subsidised
housing without creating unacceptable reductions in housing standards.
They expect to pay a reasonable proportion of their income on housing;
the fixing of rents and incessant argument over rent levels have long
ceased to be a major political issue in Scandinavia, although local disputes
can and still do occur.

Local municipalities have greater credibility and enjoy greater respect in Scandinavia than in Scotland. Considerable interest is shown in local affairs and it is interesting to note that high polls are often recorded at local elections; this in marked contrast to the derisory figures recorded at local elections in this country.

Housing co-operatives and other building groups expect and obtain a high degree of co-operation from the municipalities. They are regarded favourably by the authorities and not as rivals in the promotion of housing. In many cases, local municipalities own large areas of land surrounding towns and villages under their control. They are expected to allocate land according to the needs of the local community and to reject the socially irresponsible principle of selling land to the highest bidder – a practice which still largely decides the ownership of land for building in Scotland.

Local municipalities, housing co-operatives and private builders sponsor local and national housing competitions with surprising regularity. Each Scandinavian country promotes architectural housing competitions to advance new ideas and concepts as a matter of principle; considerable interest is shown in the results which are widely published in local and national newspapers. There have been fewer than five architectural housing competitions in the last 25 years in Scotland. The local and national press take little or no interest, and few members of the general public appreciate the value of housing competitions for promoting new ideas in house design and layout.

III Denmark

The importance of housing co-operatives and housing associations in Scandinavia has already been emphasised. The movement was started at Copenhagen in 1865 by a group of workers who joined together to form the 'Workers' Building Association' with the modest aim of providing a house for each member of the association. Members gained inspiration from the early work of the Rochdale pioneers in England, and also from a group of building workers in Edinburgh. The Danes were successful in building a number of houses for occupation by their members. They also succeeded in fostering a movement which was to exert considerable influence on other sponsors of housing throughout Scandinavia. Professor John Greve illustrates this in his book *Voluntary Housing in Scandinavia* when he says,

> The Association was of considerable significance for the development of housing associations and co-operatives. Not as a result of the number of houses built, since they were few compared to the total output

in Denmark, but by the way it stimulated interest in the improvement of housing conditions, for the lower income groups, and because its activities provided inspiration and models for subsequent
legislation.

In marked contrast to Scotland, an increasing number of housing
co-operatives began to operate successfully in Denmark during the period immediately before the First World War. These included the Workers'
Co-operative Housing Association founded in 1912 and the Workers'
Co-operative Building Association in 1913. It is significant that the
Danish government gave financial assistance to these organisations, and
actively supported them in their effort to improve housing conditions
for low-paid workers.

The First World War created a shortage of housing, causing house
rents to rise dramatically, repeating a pattern of events which occurred
in Scotland at that time. The Danish government countered these trends
by restricting rents to all existing rental property and by allocating
money to housing co-operatives and housing associations. This financial
assistance was continued into the 1920s, thus enabling the movement
to achieve a positive, if somewhat modest, success. It was not until the
beginning of the 1930s, however, that the co-operatives became sufficiently well organised to use this financial assistance really effectively.
This was largely due to a reorganisation of government policy, which
aimed at reforming and regulating the activities of housing co-operatives
and housing associations. The Housing Subsidy Act of 1933 required
all housing co-operatives and associations to be registered, and to be
vetted by a central authority, to give evidence of competence, and to
submit annual accounts for scrutiny to make certain that all state monies
given to the associations were used for legitimate house-building purposes.

Having established these principles, the government gave strong support to the non-profit housing society movement, and thus made possible
the creation of organisations which were able to promote, construct and
manage substantial numbers of good-quality homes for lower-paid workers throughout the country. Three distinct housing groups developed
during this period. First, there were the housing co-operatives which
offered a well-designed, good-quality home at cost price to potential
occupiers who were encouraged to take out shares—in many cases 5 per
cent of the cost price—in the co-operative. This entitled them to a share
in the management and also to some say in the amenity of their dwelling
and its immediate surroundings. The second group consisted of joint

stock associations which were formed to provide work for building
workers in addition to building housing. The trade union movement fig-
ured prominently in some of these organisations, becoming major shareholders and organising groups of building workers to construct houses.
These associations differed from the housing co-operatives in that they
offered houses to rent and had shareholders who did not necessarily
rent houses within the organisation. Tenants have a more limited say in
the management of an association than occupiers in a housing co-operative. The social benefit associations constituted the third group and
represented the nearest approach to council housing in Scotland. They
were formed and managed by the local authority, but differed vastly
from their Scottish counterparts in that they encouraged the formation of tenants' associations and actively consulted them on matters
of policy and management.

These non-profit societies vary considerably in size and degree of
organisation; some build on small awkward sites, restricting themselves
to programmes of under 20 houses, while some of the larger groups
build complete districts containing full community services and up to
10,000 homes covering an entire neighbourhood area. Many small
societies collaborate with national management organisations during the
planning and construction period. In this way local interests are combined with the experience and greater technical expertise of a nation-
wide organisation. Nearly 600 of these societies are scattered all over
Denmark; currently, annual production accounts for some 13,000 flats
and houses, corresponding roughly to an average of 25-30 per cent of
the total annual housing production of the country as a whole.

Some of the societies build houses and later manage and maintain
the development, while others perform only one of these operations.
Some operate in a single town; some all over the country. Others are
attached to a single building trade or local trade union. Practically all
classes of the population are represented by occupants of these houses
—except the very rich!

The initiative for starting building activities is taken by the housing
associations and not by local authorities or the government. In recent
years promoters, builders and housing authorities in Denmark have all
been concerned about continuity in housing production. This problem
is particularly important for manufacturers engaged in the production
of industrialised or pre-fabricated units for housing. Difficulties in maintaining continuity in housing construction are usually caused by the
cyclical nature of national trading patterns. In the past, the building
industry in Denmark, in common with many other countries, was first

to suffer in any trade recession; investment in building, particularly house building, was retarded and unemployment in the building industry inevitably followed. Under these circumstances it was clearly impossible to plan a continuous housing programme, particularly if such a programme made use of industrialised housing techniques.

The first tentative moves to counter this problem were made by the Danish government in 1960. A programme was set up which allowed for the construction of some 2,000 pre-fabricated houses per annum, covering a four-year period. Since 1960 this programme has been extended to cover a rolling five-year programme consisting of 7,000 subsidised housing society dwellings, 2,000 subsidised private dwellings. Under these conditions the manufacture of pre-fabricated units for housing becomes an economic proposition and manufacturers in Denmark have invested in plant and material accordingly.

In 1966, the programme received further assistance and encouragement through an agreement by the four main political parties to fix a budget and to follow an agreed housing policy for eight years regardless of any group or party which happened to be in power during this period. Latest reports show that the agreement was generally adhered to over this eight-year period. The polarity of interest in housing displayed by the main British political parties ensures that a similar kind of programme would be impossible to achieve in Britain.

Rental subsidies are available to all sections of the community in Denmark. The following is an edited version of recent government publications on the subject:

Rental subsidy is a new and modernized version of the old form of rental allowance previously operated in Denmark. Under the scheme tenants in various kinds of accommodation including non-profit housing schemes can have a proportion of the rent paid by the State in the form of a subsidy. The system applies to old and new properties alike.

The total amount of taxable income earned by the household is a vital factor in deciding whether persons are eligible for subsidy and how large the subsidy will be. If the family income has risen or fallen considerably since the last assessment, this is taken into consideration and appropriate adjustment is made. The size of the family is important because rental subsidy is granted on the principle that the greatest amount of subsidy should be allocated to large families with low incomes.

Quoting from 1971 figures, an example is given as follows:

> A family of two adults and two children rent a four-room apartment which, inclusive of maintenance, costs them 9,000 Kroner (£495) per annum. The family's total taxable income is 30,000 Kroner (£1,650). This family with two children are eligible for a rental subsidy of 3,360 Kroner (£187) per annum. Or, in other words, the family's rental expenses will be reduced from 685 Kroner (£37.68) to 405 Kroner (£22.20) every month.

Special rules apply to households comprising one adult and one child, so special rates have been compiled for this category of family. With a taxable income of 21,000 Kroner (£1,150) and a rent including maintenance of 4,000 Kroner (£220), a single person with one child would be eligible for an annual rent subsidy of 1,260 Kroner (£69.30).

Subsidy is not normally granted where there are more than two people to each living room (lounge, bedroom, etc.). In other words, two rooms equal a maximum of four persons. Local authorities can, however, grant exemption from this regulation.

There is a widespread belief that the rents of new housing accommodation are high — so high that only a few people can afford to pay. This view is in no way correct. In many instances rental subsidy slices the top off rental costs.

IV Finland

Housing co-operatives and mutual housing organisations form the largest group of housing promoters and builders in Finland; recently they were responsible for building over 50 per cent of the country's housing production. These organisations have exerted considerable influence in the formation and development of Finnish national housing policy since the late 1930s.

In the majority of Finnish housing co-operatives, an individual becomes a member of the co-operative by taking up a certain number of shares which entitle him to a permanent use of a dwelling built by the organisation to which he subscribes. The capital invested may be as little as 5-6 per cent depending on the type of organisation and method of tenure chosen by the member.

The fundamental aim of these organisations is to produce high-standard housing at reasonable costs for a broad cross-section of the population. General opinion supports the creation of residential areas where people of all social groups and professions live in close proximity. Segregated housing areas for lower-paid workers in the community find little favour in Finland.

The following table shows the degree of involvement by housing co-operatives and housing associations in the over-all house-building programme for 1975:

Housing co-operatives and housing associations built	60.3%
Private builders	24.1%
Local authorities	4.9%
Industrial builders	4.8%
Central government	0.3%
Others	5.6%
Total	100%

The Helsinki Central Housing Society, HAKA, was established on the initiative of a number of consumer co-operative organisations in the capital of the country in 1938. Thereafter, the organisation increased its scale of operations to cover the whole country. A group of private building contractors and building-material manufacturers founded the SATO organisation in 1940, which also started in the capital of the country. In 1950 a central office was created to direct the activities of the SATO organisations throughout the country. In 1951 the Housing Foundation, ASUNTOSAATIC, was established by the Finnish Family Welfare League, VAESTOLIITTO, in collaboration with five other non-profit-making associations. One of the special aims of the Housing Foundation is to create entire communities in accordance with the requirements of modern city planning. One such community is the world-famous satellite township of Tapiola which is situated on the outskirts of Helsinki. Private persons, in need of dwellings and wishing to save for their own homes, founded an association named ASUNTOSAATAJAT in 1957.

In the 1960s when a lack of rented accommodation was experienced, the trade union movement and the organisations supporting the HAKA societies founded a nation-wide co-operative society for building rented houses with the initials VVO, which produced rented dwellings primarily with the assistance of state loans. A parallel organisation was formed in 1970, when the groups supporting the SATO organisation established a joint-stock company called VATRO for the production and financing of rented dwellings.

Municipalities assist the housing co-operatives and mutual associations by subscribing for shares in the HAKA and SATO organisations by granting long-term loans for the production of houses for renting and by leasing or selling building sites to them at moderate prices. Many Finnish municipalities exert rigorous control over the allocation of suitable building land for housing in the areas under their jurisdiction. Housing co-operatives and mutual housing associations are especially favoured in this respect. Private builders have accepted, somewhat reluctantly, the need for a socially responsible policy in housing; many now tender for housing work which is sponsored by housing co-operatives and associations. In one instance, pressure by local public opinion caused builders in the Helsinki area to re-sell land to local municipalities to allow for proper design and development to take place.

Considerable financial assistance is granted by the Finnish government to assist in the construction of housing in Finland. The authority responsible for housing administration is the National Housing Board. Its activity is based on the 1966 Housing Board Act. When this law came into force the organisation which had handled housing financing activity for the state since 1949, under the name of ARAVA, was disbanded. The National Housing Board is responsible for the administration of all state loans for housing. These loans are granted either for the construction of a particular house, which is called a property-specific loan, or for a particular individual to buy a house, which is known as a personal loan. Property-specific loans are granted for the construction of rental housing, co-operative housing and mutual housing associations. Before a loan can be granted, the plans, costs and financing must be approved by the Housing Board.

The financing of rental and co-operative housing consists of housing loans from the state, and from banks using first mortgage loans granted by the state, together with the owner's own capital, or that of the members of a co-operative association. The state housing loan covers at most 60 per cent of the building costs. The interest on the loan is 1 per cent during the first five years and 3 per cent thereafter, and the amortisation term is 25 years. The first mortgage loan, which is applied for through a bank, generally covers 30 per cent of the acquisition value of the house. The interest on the loan corresponds to the general lending rate; the term of the loan is 17 years. Self-financing generally accounts for 10 per cent of the acquisition value. In the case of rented housing, this share is paid by the owner. Occupants of co-operative dwellings contribute this share as a co-operative charge before moving into the dwelling.

The financing of mutual housing associations consists of a state loan, a first mortgage granted by a bank and the shareholders' own capital. The state housing loan covers a maximum of 30 per cent of the building costs. The interest is 3 per cent and the term of the loan 25 years. The first mortgage loan covers 30-35 per cent of the acquisition value of the house. The interest corresponds to the general lending rate and the term is 17 years. Self-financing by the purchasers of the dwellings covers 35-40 per cent of the acquisition value and may consist of the cash capital of the owner augmented by a personal loan from the state and a reciprocal loan granted by some banks.

Personal loans granted by the state for the purchase of a dwelling form a parallel system to that of property-specific loans granted to housing companies. Personal loans may not be granted for the purchase of a dwelling in a house which has already been subsidised by the state; and the plans, costs and financing of the house in question must be approved by the Housing Board. Since state loans for dwellings in these housing companies are granted to those occupants who are considered to be most in need of such help, the system is in this respect more flexible than that of property-specific loans. The state personal housing loan covers at most 30 per cent of the building costs. The interest is 3 per cent and the term of the loan from 15 to 25 years depending on the recipient's means. Persons in even greater need may receive an additional personal loan from the state; these loans may be granted for the acquisition of a dwelling in a house already subsidised by a state housing loan, or in a house without such subsidy in connection with the regular personal loan.

The additional loan covers a maximum of 30 per cent of the building costs of the dwelling or house, depending on the means and income of the recipient. Amortisation begins only after eight years, during which period it is free of interest. After that the interest rate is 3 per cent and the amortisation period from 9 to 25 years depending on the borrower's income and means.

The applicant's income is assessed on the basis of his annual taxable income and that of his family. The relevant income limits are set annually by the National Housing Board and they are defined in terms both of the number of persons in the family and of the size of the dwelling. Income may also be defined in terms of taxable monthly income.

V Sweden

There are three main building agencies in Sweden: 'public utility' companies, housing co-operatives and private builders. The public utility companies are sponsored and controlled by local municipalities who are also entitled to appoint directors to the board. Private builders and other organisations usually build for these companies; an interesting exception is the Stockholm company of Svenska Bostäder which was largely responsible for the promotion and construction of the well-known satellite township of Vällingby outside Stockholm. The public utility companies account for roughly 40 per cent of Swedish housing production. Housing co-operatives are non-profit-making bodies which build houses for members to occupy on a basis of joint ownership. Two of the largest and most influential of these organisations are described below. The co-operatives are responsible for some 15 per cent of Swedish housing production. Private enterprise builds houses for sale and flats for letting. Surprisingly enough, it is almost entirely financed with the aid of government loans. Some 40 per cent of the total housing output is constructed in this manner.

The following is a brief description of two of the largest and most influential housing co-operatives in Sweden.

In 1923, a group was formed under the name of the Tenants' Savings and Building Society, more commonly known now by the initials HSB. This organisation has become one of the largest and most influential housing agencies in Sweden with a membership of over 20,000 and a responsibility for 200 housing co-operatives. The HSB is particularly interesting in that it combines savings, construction and management within a single organisation. A series of 'mother' co-operatives were formed to cover specific areas all over Sweden. These units were and are still responsible for planning new building operations, for encouraging their members to save, for acquiring building land—usually from the local municipality—and for supervising construction of housing.

The organisation works in the following way: on completion of a housing contract, the 'mother' society organises local members into a 'daughter' society which takes over the houses and becomes responsible for all administration, management and maintenance services. The 'mother' co-operative has still, however, to ensure that the 'daughter' co-operatives carry out these services in accordance with the rules of the organisation. The 'daughter' group owns the group of buildings under its control. The occupants are neither tenants nor are they owners; each member is entitled to indefinite occupancy provided he makes regular payments and abides by the rules of the society. The 'daughter' society is governed by ordinary members who elect representatives to the board of the association. At national level there is a central board the members of which are democratically elected from the 'mother' societies. They are responsible for policy and amendments to the constitution within the HSB.

The main functions of the HSB are now summarised as follows: to organise and to promote savings among members of the organisation, to provide loans and to offer legal and technical assistance to 'mother' societies, to purchase building materials at wholesale prices and to make arrangements to produce building materials and, finally, to promote the exchange of new ideas between the various established groups within the organisation and to form new co-operatives where required by local people.

In order to finance building operations, the HSB set up its own banking organisation. The personal savings of members are handled by the bank to finance an appreciable part of the construction costs incurred by 'mother' societies. The bank is also able to negotiate credit from other services to finance building operations. Specialised departments have been created to provide first-class administration, architectural and planning advisory services. Another important aspect of the organisation is concerned with research. The HSB has acquired valuable knowledge on all aspects of housing promotion and construction from nearly 50 years of operational experience. This explains why housing co-operatives were able to introduce advanced methods of construction more readily than comparable private building groups; they were among the first in Europe to produce large building components constructed in timber or concrete which are normally built up laboriously on site. Complete kitchen and bathroom units are also manufactured to reduce site labour costs and construction time. These items are produced in factories owned by the organisation. The HSB also set up factories to manufacture basic components such as bricks, cement, doors and windows to supply its own needs and also those of others, including private contractors. These groups were formed to improve standards of production and marketing at competitive rates and to break manufacturing kartels within the building supply industry.

The original groups who were responsible for forming the HSB organisations realised that little could be achieved without adequate financial backing. A savings system was instituted and the HSB was given the authority to function as a commercial bank. Higher interest rates than those normally given by commercial banking institutions were paid to subscribers to encourage the growth of the organisation. Not all of the subscribers were members; some were merely investors, while others saved to improve an existing home or to obtain a larger home within the organisation. In this way the HSB was able to function effectively; it could now buy land and finance building work and was able to pursue a policy of continuing expansion and development.

Another organisation called Svenska Rikbyggen, known by the initials SR, was formed by a number of building trade unions to combat rising unemployment in the building industry during the Second World War.

Four major building trade unions were responsible initially for setting up the enterprise. The original group was joined by the Swedish Confederation of Trade Unions and also by a number of trade union-owned industrial and commercial enterprises. The controlling interest in the organisation is still, however, held by the four original unions. The SR grew rapidly after 1945 to share an equally dominant role with the HSB in the Swedish post-war housing programme. By 1951 the organisation could confidently set up a financial section to borrow money from individual unions to provide operational and investment capital for house-building programmes.

The organisation of the SR is very similar to the HSB in many respects; national, regional and local groups exist to carry out roughly the same functions as their equivalents in the HSB: bulk buying and the hiring of plant and equipment follow roughly similar patterns. A comprehensive planning and design service is offered to member groups within the organisation and, again, research and development services are available.

An important aspect of the work of the SR is concerned with the provision of rented housing for local municipalities. The SR is invited to provide a design and construction service. A non-profit housing association is set up in which the local municipality and the SR take equal shares. This partnership is known as a semi-public organisation in which the SR still retains an interest once the construction programme has been completed. In another situation, the local municipality sponsors and takes over the management of the completed contract. This is the nearest equivalent to local authority housing in Sweden.

After the Second World War the Swedish government decided to rationalise existing national housing policies. A positive programme of financial assistance was passed by the legislature to assist house-building organisations to improve housing standards and to reduce overcrowding in the larger towns and cities. The housing co-operative movement, public utility companies and private enterprise all benefited in this respect.

A general description of the method used to finance housing construction in Sweden is as follows:

Public utility companies, co-operatives and private contractors can obtain first and second mortgage loans in the private market, from savings banks, mortgage banks and insurance companies to cover normally 70 per cent of the total cost. The County Board then make a third loan, carrying the greatest risk, so that in theory private builders can borrow a total of 85 per cent, co-operatives 95 per cent and local authorities and public utility companies 100 per cent. In practice the loans are often less than these proportions, because the government has laid down maximum figures of cost for different types of houses in different parts of the country. If the actual cost exceeds the approved limit, the loan will be calculated on the lower figure, so that the prospective builder has to find the balance himself, as an increase of his deposit.

The interest rate on the government's third loan is 4 per cent, which represents a considerable subsidy, because the government has to pay more than this for its own borrowing. Moreover, to prevent temporary fluctuations of interest rates from discouraging building and increasing rents, the government has undertaken to cover any interest payments in excess of certain limits. For houses started since January 1958 these limits are 3½ per cent on first mortgage loans and 4 per cent on second mortgage.

State subsidised loans have thus been available to all builders and building agencies without any test of financial needs, and the great majority of all new dwellings built since the war have been financed in this way. For non-profit housing – whether by local authorities, public utility companies or co-operatives – the loans do not carry any restrictions as to the rent that may be charged, but a private builder who is helped by a government loan is bound to charge a rent no higher than a limit fixed by the County Board. The limit is calculated to cover the running costs and the average annual cost of repayment of capital and interest and to provide the builder with a return on the share of the total capital which was invested by him – normally 15 per cent of total approved building costs, as he can get total loans of up to 85 per cent of this cost. The return on his investment works out at 5 per cent in the first year, but as the years pass the interest which he has to pay decreases and, as rents remain the same, the yield on his invested capital will increase.

The government also helps indirectly to finance housing projects by assisting people with rental subsidies which vary according to income and family circumstances. Protection is also offered to borrowers in the event of any rise in the interest rates imposed on first and second mortgages. The difference between the initial rate and any new rate of interest is usually made up by a supplementary payment on the third mortgage or state loan.

An interesting change in the conditions relating to state loans was made in 1968; previously to these repayment costs on a state loan were made at a standard rate of interest over a period of 30 years. Under the new scheme repayments were made at a low rate during the initial years, gradually rising over the period to ensure the elimination of both capital and interest debt during the thirtieth year. This alteration was meant to ensure that repayment costs could be related to current building costs over the loan period. It also ensured that these repayments were not subjected to the fluctuations of market interest rates, thus eliminating the need to subsidise first and second mortgages.

Another Act passed by the Swedish government in 1968 was concerned with the acquisition of building land by local municipalities. The idea was to ensure that an adequate supply of land would be made available to meet housing requirements in the foreseeable future. A special government loan fund was set up to assist local municipalities to purchase suitable land for building houses in and around the urban areas. The basis of these land transactions was concerned with agreed purchase between the municipality and the seller as opposed to the long-drawn and often traumatic practices of compulsory purchase.

VI

From this brief description, it would appear that housing problems in Scandinavia are minimal, and that a near-utopian housing situation exists in these countries; this is not so, and it would certainly be wrong if this impression were given. Housing problems and shortages do occur in the Nordic states, especially in the larger towns and cities; some unfortunate people are given little choice in housing and many have to wait for a considerable period before obtaining a house. Undue emphasis and priority have been given to high-rise housing projects in some Scandinavian housing programmes; some of the new neighbourhood areas are characterised by monotonous filing-cabinet blocks, which are reminiscent of many recent Scottish high-rise developments in form, if not in detail.

The over-all quality of housing is excellent, but in many cases the size of the accommodation provided in relation to family size is small — house areas were, until comparatively recently, smaller than the equivalent house areas provided by local authorities in Scotland. This has resulted in severe overcrowding in some parts of Scandinavia; Stockholm and Malmö in Sweden have been, and still are, particularly affected in this respect. The cost of accommodation is high for most sections of the community — up to 30 per cent of taxable income — and as a result many wives feel obliged to take jobs when their children are still very small or in other equally inconvenient circumstances.

A high percentage of the population, currently living in the towns and cities, are housed in flats, although many would really prefer to live at ground level with the option of having a garden. Many houses, suitable for conversion and upgrading in the inner town areas, have been demolished; some of these have been torn down to make way for new office blocks, thus often repeating the pattern of irresponsible commercial development which has also recently taken place in Scotland.

Severe criticisms have been made about government housing policies and government interference in matters concerned with housing; some critics maintain that housing problems have been increased by government intervention; others believe that housing subsidies and all other forms of government assistance should be discontinued altogether.

In spite of these drawbacks and disagreements, however, it is obvious that housing policies and programmes both in Sweden and in Scandinavia as a whole are considerably in advance of the measures taken by successive British governments to alleviate housing problems in Scotland. It is also clear that attitudes, expectations and values in Scandinavia are very different from those which currently find favour in Scotland.

4

HOUSING IN THE PUBLIC SECTOR

It was the 1919 Government Housing Act which really gave impetus to
the development and construction of council housing in Scotland. By
imposing on local authorities a specific duty to provide for general housing needs, the government made provision for direct state intervention
in the housing market. This decision has exerted a profound influence
on the general condition and appearance of the domestic environment
in Scotland for over fifty years. It was during this period that the local
authorities became the principal promoters of housing in Scotland. While
it is true to say that private developers and builders were given some incentive by the Chamberlain Act of 1923 to provide housing for renting
to lower-paid workers, the idea gained little support and in the end had
to be abandoned. It appeared that private enterprise was no longer
interested in building houses for working people in Scotland.

Council housing became an integral part of the Scottish urban scene;
it became an institution – an enshrined shibboleth in the minds of many
people. Once established, no one seemed seriously to doubt or question
the validity or desirability of promoting large municipal housing programmes, or even troubled to investigate alternative methods of subsidised housing promotion. Apparently, this was the only workable
method of subsidising house building in Scotland. Yet, increasingly,
many local authority housing developments, particularly those located
on the periphery of larger burgh and city areas, are proving to be an
expensive, unsatisfactory and highly inefficient way of housing people
in Scotland.

Much has already been written on the subject, and little is to be gained
by tiresome reiteration of well-worn themes. Certain aspects of local
authority housing organisation and housing programmes do bear closer
and more critical examination, however, and it is now proposed to dis-
cuss them briefly under a series of headings as follows.

Promotion

Enlightened promotion is an important and significant factor in all successful housing developments both at home and abroad. It is most effective
when carried out by persons and organisations who have a well-developed
sense of social responsibility, a genuine desire to improve housing standards
and a need to create a better domestic environment. Energy and determin-

1. Tenements at Hyndland, Glasgow. Architects: John McKellar and C.J. McNair.

2. The Study, Culross.

3. Terraced Housing at Delft, Holland. Architect: Herman Hertzberger.

4. Flats at Otaharju near Helsinki, Finland. Architect: Heikki Kaija Siren.

5. Terraced Housing at Moss Park, Glasgow. Architect: Glasgow Council.

6. Mixed Development at Cowcaddens, Glasgow. Architects: Walter Underwood & Ptrs.

7. Private Housing at Marly Green, North Berwick. Architect: Calthorpe and Mars. (Photograph by Inglis Stevens.)

8. Great Western Terrace, Glasgow. Architect: Alexander Thomson.

9. Flats at Comiston, Edinburgh. Architect: James Gray.

10. Flats and Maisonettes at Bridgend, Perth. Architects: James Parr & Ptrs.

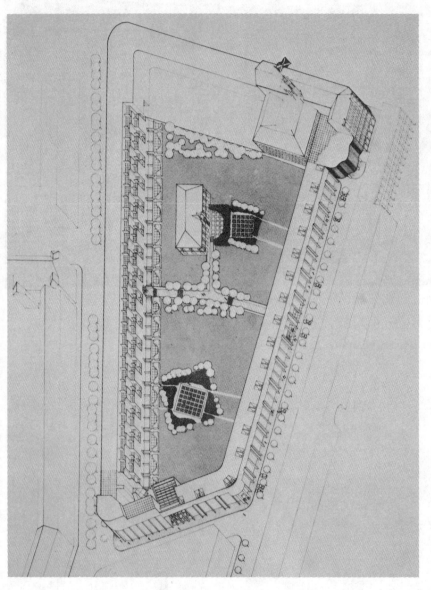

11. Proposed Urban Renewal at Raeberry Street, Woodside, Glasgow. Student: Tommy Thomson, Tutor: Douglas Niven.

ation are also required to carry out satisfactory solutions to complex housing problems, to ensure that value for money is obtained and also that the highest possible standards in house building are observed. How does the average Scottish local authority measure up to these exacting requirements?

From the beginning (1920), many local authorities were extremely reluctant to implement the new housing Acts; some authorities simply did not want to become involved in the housing market, claiming lack of expertise and lack of resources to meet expected commitments; others objected strongly, reasoning that business would be taken from speculative builders and others concerned in the building industry, and that these organisations were much better qualified to build houses than the local authority. It was also argued that local voting patterns would be altered by building council houses in certain areas and that migrant workers might be attracted to new housing developments. Delays in implementing and carrying forward local authority housing programmes were common; trivial reasons were often found to explain unsatisfactory progress. These attitudes created a tradition of reluctant action which is hardly dispelled to this day in some parts of Scotland.

In addition, the composition and organisation of a local authority appears to work in opposition to the creation of satisfactory housing promotion in Scotland. The 'directors' of the local authority housing agency are a group of elected councillors called the Housing Committee. These 'directors' may, or may not, be the initiators of local authority housing programmes. A variety of 'initiators' were suggested to the author: these were the local sanitary inspector, the housing manager, the burgh factor, chief architect, burgh surveyor, burgh chamberlain and, finally, the chief planner. In some local authorities, no one really seemed to know who initiated a housing development. Members of housing committees are necessarily concerned about local housing problems; many are certainly not interested in good housing design, or in the creation of satisfactory house layout plans. The activities of many housing committees are questionable, and are certainly not always directed towards the proper promotion of consistent and well-considered housing programmes. Some members of committees appear to operate in an obstructive, or negative capacity. Considerable delays may be caused by political party group manoeuvring, or personal manoeuvring, both in committee and in open council meetings. Predictably, indifferent decisions are taken and erratic progress occurs; developments can be delayed, curtailed or postponed indefinitely in areas where genuine need for housing exists. In some cases, the promotion of housing is actually being inhibited by the 'promoters'

of the local housing agency. The members of these committees also face
the embarrassing problem of having to satisfy local electorates. Paradox-
ically, however, decisions on housing are taken without proper consultation of local people who are most likely to be affected by any new proposals or redevelopment.

The principal local authority officials who act as executive officers
to housing committees are faced with a difficult situation; the successful promotion of housing projects determined by a housing committee
is certainly not an easy task. It requires a man of considerable talent,
dedication, even will-power, to give reasoned advice and to interpret
decisions made by many housing committees. Such individuals are rare
in the architecture and planning departments of local authorities in
Scotland. Not surprisingly, many give up the unequal struggle and settle
for a 'quiet life'. This attitude in turn leads to disillusion amongst the
senior officers and to apathetic indifference within the lower ranks of
many departments. In this atmosphere, many simply become architectural 'time servers'. The essential dedication required for the vital task
of creating a decent housing environment is dissipated; initiative and
creativity are stifled or simply disappear altogether. It is hardly surprising,
therefore, that many local authority architectural and planning offices in
Scotland operate at a very low key, producing work which at best is safe
and stereotyped and, at worst, dreary, boring and an affront to civilised
man.

Segregation

Speculative builders and developers of the Victorian period achieved
remarkable variety in house building during the great building booms
in the latter half of the nineteenth century. An interesting juxtaposition
of differing housing types was quite common; groups of large detached
villas, terraced villas and tenemental properties often shared conter-
minous boundaries; five or six differing house types could be built within
a half-mile radius of each other. The layout of these houses provides a
lesson in domestic urban planning which is not fully appreciated by developers, planners and architects to this day.

One practical reason for these highly successful groupings was concerned with land sales; during the nineteenth century, plots of land
considered suitable for building purposes were sold off in small lots and
to a variety of potential developers. There was also a greater number of
builders concerned in house building during the Victorian period. In
effect, this allowed varying income groups to live in reasonable proximity,
ensured that local communities covered a wider spectrum of society, and

also gave considerable interest to the urban scene. In direct contrast to this, most council housing developments were designed in self-contained groups, separated from neighbouring communities and built in such a way that it is impossible to make provision for other types of housing development within the boundary of any such area. The vast scale of many developments did not help to create a variety of housing layout. In many areas, local authorities acquired substantial quantities of land for building houses and, as they became the sole house-building agency in many districts, little variety and contrast in housing types could be expected.

But perhaps the most significant factor which resulted from this kind of development was the creation of clearly defined physical areas where people from lower-income groups were expected or even directed to live. Many were isolated from the rest of the community; some developments in fact appear to have been specially designed with segregation in mind. These developments have added a highly divisive physical dimension to the social class structure in Scotland. The deletion of all references to 'working classes' in the Housing Scotland Act of 1949 made little significant difference to the general appearance of council housing areas, or to the status of the occupants. The damage had already been done—the lines of demarcation were now complete between housing in the public and private sectors.

Choice

An important aspect of housing in any country is concerned with the degree of choice which is available in the types of living accommodation. In an ideal situation, the following determinants of choice would be fully considered: location (desirability of place and relation to work and to public services), cost, tenure and facilities within the house (space, design, equipment, condition). Obviously, few people are able to consider these determinants in full, and it is widely accepted that a compromise situation is normal and inevitable. Choice in housing is largely determined by economic purchasing power and stable employment or, to put it more bluntly, by money. In this respect choice in housing is still largely a middle-class prerogative.

In Scotland a total lack of choice exists in many areas; this was caused by low earning capacity, by unstable employment and by traditional reluctance by Scottish people to pay for adequate living accommodation. These factors have consistently restricted the choice of housing which can be made available to the average family in Scotland. A highly unsatisfactory situation has resulted. The size and type of house constructed in Scotland is largely determined by others—mainly by local authorities.

Returning to the 'model' for choice and relating it to a situation in which the local authority acts as the main provider of housing in a given area, the following pattern emerges. Location: choice is often severely restricted to one, two, or three choices in predetermined neighbourhoods. Freedom of choice in this respect may depend on the capacity of an individual to wait from 5 to 12 years for a house in a favoured area. Cost: does not apply, see under tenure. Tenure: restricted to renting only — there are a few isolated exceptions where outright sale to sitting tenants is permitted. Facilities: the amount of space for any local authority house is determined by central government departments, this also applies to cost. Design: this is proposed by architects and planners and decided by members of housing committees and by the Scottish Development Department. Any additional equipment provided in the house is agreed by the housing committee and, finally, the condition and appearance of the property is determined by the management and maintenance departments of the local authority. It must be painfully obvious from this brief analysis that choice in local authority housing is so restricted and so improperly controlled that it may be largely discounted altogether. For many, in Scotland, choice in housing simply does not exist.

In a situation where reasonable choice exists, i.e. at least some of the determinants of choice may be observed, local authorities will be faced with the problem of empty and unwanted property—this situation obtains already in some Scottish cities and burghs. No one, except the very rich, willingly lives at a density of 120-150 persons to the acre— although many planners, architects and councillors still believe that these densities are necessary, or even desirable. Few choose to live in multi-storey blocks if reasonable alternatives are available at a lower level. Nobody seeks to live beside noisy freeways, clearance areas, main-line railways or large industrial complexes—local authority houses are often situated in close proximity to highly unsuitable areas. Few willingly make a home on a peripheral city site which offers minimum public services or totally inadequate public transport.

The position is well summed up by Nicholas Taylor in his book *The Village in the City*, when he says

the dishonesty of fashionable architects who sit all day at their drawing boards at County Hall designing harsh piazzas for Battersea and Bermondsey, and then at 4.51 pm sharp descend into the tube train, roaring out under the forgotten Redevelopment Areas for which they are responsible, until they come to the surface at their own cosy creeper hung cottages in Hampstead and Wimbledon.

The city quoted is in England, and it is the architect who is specifically singled out for castigation; these strictures could equally well apply to a Scottish city and to many of the surveyors, engineers and planners, and to many local councillors, national politicians and senior civil servants who are responsible for housing programmes in Scotland.

Motivation

Since 1919, housing has become the subject of major political statements by the main political parties in Scotland; it has become an integral part of government policy. Many governments in Western Europe are also committed in one way or another to the principle of a national housing policy and most Europeans now accept the inevitability of government intervention in the housing market.

The problem of government intervention in Scotland is greatly aggravated by the polarity of interest displayed by the major political parties both at local and national levels. Housing acts as a powerful bargaining counter in that it is one of the few tangible objects a politician can offer, or appear to offer, to his constituents in Scotland. This attractive bargaining device has been used to considerable advantage by politicians of all persuasions. It is perhaps significant that the most important committees in many local councils are the housing and planning committees.

A bewildering number of Housing Acts have been added to the statute book since 1919; these Acts have, in many cases, reflected the political beliefs of the major political parties; none of them has offered, or could offer, positive solutions to Scottish housing 'problems'. These 'problems' have still to be analysed and quantified. The true extent of housing 'need' in Scotland is still largely unknown, while 'demand' for housing has always been severely restricted by an embarrassing lack of purchasing power.

At national level, housing programmes have been distorted, delayed or even improperly advanced despite a continuing and genuine housing need. In these circumstances the creation of a coherent national housing programme becomes impossible. In spite of many protestations to the contrary, housing in Scotland continues to enjoy a low priority in government strategy. Successive British governments have taken this attitude since the end of the Second World War, and show little sign of their altering priorities now or in the immediate future. At local level, the polarising of political attitudes in the main cities and burghs has had a disastrous effect on housing standards, and on the general appearance of the domestic environment in Scotland.

An acute shortage of houses after the Second World War engendered a predictable myopia among local politicians; it became essential to think of housing simply in terms of numbers. Success in local politics was in fact measured by the number of housing units produced by an administration. Long-term investment potential, quality, maintenance and the provision of attendant social and commercial services were either ignored or given low priority in many housing programmes. It was somehow imagined that these services could be added at a later date. It was also believed that little harm would be caused by the lack of these facilities in new housing areas. The consequences of this misguided policy are now obvious to all concerned with housing problems in Scotland.

Permissions

One of the most frustrating aspects of municipal housing development is concerned with time-consuming bureaucratic processes which occur both at national and at local levels before work can begin on site. While the average house-building contract may take between 18 months and 24 months to complete, the average time taken to obtain all permissions to build may take up to five years or more.

The first problem in the pre-contract period deals with the acquisition of land to build houses. A discerning local authority will make provision for this by anticipating future projected housing requirements. The process of purchasing land and obtaining permission to purchase land is often difficult and not at all popular with many local officials who are engaged in land and property acquisition. Considerable delays may also be experienced by the unnecessarily complicated process of getting permission to build from the local authority council. Housing layout plans are frequently shuttled backwards and forwards between full council, political party group, housing committee and housing sub-committee to the extreme bewilderment of staff in architectural or planning departments. This process may take many months, it may even take years, depending on the position of the site, the degree of opposition met from members of the committee and the depth of personal interest shown by individual councillors.

Provided approvals are obtained locally, the next problem is to obtain permission from the government representative in Scotland; this body is called the Scottish Development Department. At least three permissions are required before work on site can begin. A fast time for the first permission – preliminary approvals – might be two months or possibly three; a longer time might be as much as nine months.

The second approval – detail proposals with estimated costs – might take a month, or it could take up to twelve months, depending on the current political and economic climate. In the fifties and sixties during the classic period of 'stop-go' in the management of the British economy, the Treasury ruled that approvals for local authority housing in Scotland be withheld during a 'stop' period; it then ordered the Development Department to perform a complete *volte-face* a few months later by encouraging the same authorities to proceed with indecent haste with individual housing projects during a period of 'go'. This policy obviously had a disastrous effect on the continuity of local authority housing programmes and also greatly reduced morale in many architectural and planning departments. In a 'stop' situation architects were repeatedly asked by the Development Department in Edinburgh to make petty changes to housing developments submitted for approval; this device was used as a delaying tactic to conserve government expenditure on housing. This sedate 'charade' between architect and department could be acted out over a period of many months.

In a period of 'go', local authority architectural departments had difficulty in dealing with the sudden increase in the work load and were obliged to 'farm out' housing projects to others. These projects were often taken up by building contractors offering an 'all-in' service – known as a 'package deal'. These 'packages' of housing proved eminently suitable for the production of a maximum number of units in the shortest possible time. Naturally, contractors offering these services became very popular with many local housing committees who appreciated projects which emphasised quantity above all else.

During the third approval stage – submission of builders' estimates – all manner of delaying tactics are possible. Costs which are estimated to be over the approved limit – the upper limit on these costs remained firmly behind a bureaucratic cloud in Scotland until 1967 when an 'indicative cost' (in England the 'cost yardstick') for government-financed housing was first introduced – present department officials with a heaven-sent opportunity to refer, or to delay, approvals for an indefinite period. Approvals may take two months if costs are within the current indicative cost ratings – a highly unlikely situation, particularly during a period of rising inflation – and between six and nine months if costs are unacceptable to the Department.

Finally, certain costs connected with the housing account have to be spent within a given financial year, otherwise the local authority loses the right to gain benefit from these funds. In this situation, ill-considered decisions may be made by local councils and money may be squandered

for no good reason apart from the necessity of complying with an inflexible and meaningless bureaucratic time-scale.

Speculation

A high-rise subsidy granted by the government for multi-storey flat construction in the late fifties prompted the building industry in Scotland
to invest in plant and materials for high-rise construction. Many local
authority councillors, architects, engineers and planners endorsed the
idea of high-rise house building with enthusiasm. For some, the political
symbolism of the 'multi' had an overpowering attraction – in this way
an instant high-density living could be achieved with the minimum of
inconvenience and with the maximum of ostentation. For those who
should have known better, the technology of building high seemed to
blind all other considerations. Others were simply impressed by elegant
representations of multi-storey buildings in model form – a purely visual
approach.

The major building contractors naturally viewed the subsidy in rather
more practical terms: here for the first time was a real opportunity to
extract maximum profitability from local authority housing construction.
Contractors were not to be blamed for taking this attitude – an opportunity had been given and was seized with alacrity. Unfortunately, the
whole business got somewhat out of hand; contractors quickly devised a 'package deal contract' for multi-storey flats; this offered a
complete planning, design and building service for housing development.
To the layman, it must have seemed an attractive proposition – x number
of houses erected in y number of months for z number of pounds – all
very simple. Soon the burgh and city council buildings in many parts of
central Scotland were besieged by contractors' representatives touting
multi-storey blocks in much the same way as door-to-door salesmen sell
vacuum cleaners to housewives. These representatives simply requested
that a site – any site, however inappropriate – be allocated to them and
all would be well. The tiresome business of obtaining competitive tenders,
paying professional fees and many other attendant problems would be
avoided and the whole operation completed with a minimum of inconvenience to councillors and to local authority officials.

Local authority architects and planners viewed the 'package deal' idea
with mixed feelings; for some, it was a godsend – it relieved them of a
great deal of the responsibility for housing in their area. Others were
suspicious of contracts of this nature and regarded them as an intrusion
in their field of operations; it was argued that competition was unfair,
in that contractors' design teams were less nice minded about where and

how they designed and built housing. Some officials openly opposed this highly seductive method of providing housing in bulk, but many had little success and were often castigated for their pains.

It is difficult to estimate the number of houses produced in Scotland by the 'package deal' method; during the hey-day of the 'package deal' in the mid sixties, figures of over 50 per cent of the total housing production might have been appropriate.

The Scottish Development Department adopted a curious attitude towards the 'package deal' type of contract; little or no differentiation was made between 'package deal' and traditional tendering methods. In other words, the Department appeared to raise no objection to the principle of the 'package deal' provided the cost came within the housing indicative cost limits. With few safeguards at local level or at national level, multi-storey flats were built on highly inappropriate sites in burghs and cities throughout Scotland. Even small burghs could hardly resist the temptation to build a set of high blocks. These developments were concerned with prestige and status and had little to do with the basic principles of good domestic planning.

Deterioration

Incalculable social and environmental damage was caused by gross overcrowding in urban areas during the nineteenth century. Equally disturbing, though less fully appreciated, were the disastrous effects of many local authority housing policies in the post-war era. At the end of the Second World War politicians in many local authorities—especially in the West of Scotland—believed that a complete programme of municipalisation of all privately rented housing was possible and politically desirable. Some even believed that all houses in a burgh or city should be owned by the local authority. This ridiculous notion, coupled with existing policies of excessive rent control and high rates, ensured that many properties, including many reasonable tenemental properties, could only deteriorate beyond repair. The rehabilitation of existing pre-1914 houses was made more difficult by the combination of these unrealistic attitudes.

During the 1950s and 1960s, some attempts were made by housing associations and other charitable bodies to take over and restore older domestic property in burghs and cities. The necessary permissions and funds for these operations could only be obtained through the good offices of local authorities; their response to the associations was almost entirely negative. Superficially, the reason given for the rejection of many applications was a lack of suitable funds. In reality, the associations were regarded as rivals to the local authority house-building programmes and as such could not be tolerated; this narrow-minded attitude ensured that little could be done by these associations in the urban areas.

It was not until the passing of the Housing Act in 1969 that the potential of older housing as a source of 'new' housing supply was fully appreciated. The Act allowed for payments to be made for rehabilitation of older housing which was considered suitable for conversion and up-grading. This applied equally to private and to council house properties. Unfortunately, the Act came too late to stave off advanced environmental decay in many areas. The damage had already been done; communities were scattered; bombsite conditions were created for those condemned to remain. Demolition programmes, sponsored by local sanitary departments, were considerably in advance of the faltering programmes of re-development initiated by local planners. Many plans were delayed or postponed due to Treasury 'stops', or by the reasonable objections of local people to highly questionable planning proposals. Current programmes of housing redevelopment are often spaced over a period of twenty years or more. This time-scale is hardly relevant for a young mother in her early twenties or for a child of ten. New generations are presently being raised in Scotland under conditions which should not be tolerated by a civilised society.

Paternalism

For those who suffer from unstable employment, who earn low wages, or who believe that they cannot or indeed should not own property, the alternative—in a situation where housing for renting in the private sector is rapidly disappearing—is to rent a house from a local authority. Where the local authority acts as landlord there is a natural tendency, commonly held by many socially minded organisations, to believe that they know what is best for their tenants. The absence of any real alternative to municipally rented housing in Scotland allows Scottish local authorities to indulge themselves to the full in this belief. In turn, the tenant expects the council to be a universal provider—a kind of municipal fairy godmother. This paternalistic relationship is unhealthy, anachronistic and, in the end, undignified for both parties.

There are some aspects of this paternalism which bear closer examination. In this respect, a visit to a local housing manager's department is instructive; some offices bear a remarkable similarity to old-time labour exchanges; in others the physical trappings of an egalitarian society hardly conceal a veiled 'take it or leave it' attitude which emanates from behind the counter. For those who, for one reason or another, cannot aspire to middle-class norms of behaviour, the outlook from the waiting room is bleak indeed.

A prospective tenant is often faced with a restricted choice or even, in some cases, practically no choice at all. In any event, if he 'gets a house', he has to sign a form setting out his obligations to the council; these may be altered at any time and without notice. The council is not obliged to set out its obligations to tenants. The tenant is made to feel that a favour has been granted, that he has been given a 'hand-out', and that he should be eternally grateful to the authority for putting a roof over his head.

'In the field' the situation is little better; admittedly, once a key is taken, a council house is to all intents and purposes 'owned' by the tenant for life. Many tenants, not unnaturally, attempt to prove this by making extensive improvements or by adding expensive accessories to the property. Nothing, however, can alter the fact that the council may inspect, assess conditions, or even repossess the house at any time, or that the rent of a lifetime is paid for no return at all! In many areas notices abound exhorting negative responses: no loitering, no football, no children and so on. In general, local authority factorage simply requires that the rent be paid and the rules be obeyed.

The formation of tenants' associations in local authority areas is at best a haphazard affair; privately, some authorities regard a tenants' association as a nuisance and do little to promote or to encourage the formation of such groups. Many local authority areas have no tenants' associations to make representation to the council on matters which affect local communities and no criteria by which they can judge the standard of the facilities offered in a particular district. Collective responsibility in a recognisable 'village' or local sense is positively discouraged by mindless factorage and by the inflexibility of an entrenched system.

Local authority paternalism also discourages the formation of local self-help groups: consider, for example, a situation in which local tenants have formed a group to build a long-awaited nursery school cum community centre on a piece of vacant land owned by the council. The idea is of course ridiculous, but is it? And why should this be, if official provision for the school or community centre cannot be made for 20 or 30 years?

Yet another and possibly more frightening aspect of this misguided paternalism is concerned with the attitudes of officials in the local authority departments of engineering, architecture and planning. It is here that the 'we know best' syndrome is given physical dimension.

Designs are created in isolation and without concern for the needs and wishes of the prospective tenants. That architects and planners are able to indulge themselves in this ridiculous way is due to the hopelessly compromised position of their 'clients' who are not allowed and who do not expect to be involved in the planning or design of housing or its surroundings; they have been conditioned over many years of unstable employment and excessive high-density living to wait patiently and –until very recently –accept what they were given with gratitude and little complaint. It is a bad situation –a situation in which the prospective tenants are unable to express their needs or to influence design procedures; in turn, architects and planners cannot function effectively without the advice of 'live clients'. The professionals desperately need to be properly informed about local opinion and to learn to appreciate the requirements and aspirations of local communities. Elected local authority representatives have proved conclusively over many years that they are unable to act effectively in this matter. The nineteenth-century paternalism of the private landlord has simply been replaced by his twentieth-century counterpart in the municipal buildings.

Allocation

One of the most controversial issues –apart from the problem of house rents –in the council housing sector is concerned with the allocation of houses to prospective tenants. Many local authority schemes do not enjoy public confidence, in that they do not appear to follow definite or recognisable rules. Some authorities still operate a cumbersome points system, while in others the rules of allocation appear to be incomprehensible to ordinary people. The situation is not improved by the well-established belief that certain privileged individuals appear to 'jump the housing queue', or are able to exchange an old house for a new one with comparative ease.

Remarkable variations occur in the waiting time before a house can be allocated to an applicant; in 1972 the shortest time was about one month for houses which were situated in highly undesirable areas, rising by varying degrees to twelve years for houses in highly acceptable areas. In the cities a curious debilitating stamina is certainly required to obtain a council house in a desirable area. Normally, however, the applicant with the best chance of 'topping the list' is a middle-aged man who has lived in the same area for many years, has three or more children, enjoys poor health and lives in condemned property. If this example is to be taken as a model, then prospects for a fit, newly married man in his twenties are very poor indeed.

Another disturbing aspect of local authority allocation policies is concerned with residential qualification, i.e. the time an applicant may have to wait before his name can be added to a council list: in some cases the waiting time may be a year, but it can be longer in some districts. Official government policy favours the abolition of residential qualification as an instrument in the determination of housing requirement; many local authorities, unfortunately, do not seem to share this view. The validity of the residential qualification is highly questionable in that it deliberately discourages mobility – particularly job mobility. Many are discouraged from seeking alternative employment in other areas of the country in case they lose a place on a local housing list. It is in fact easier to move out of the country altogether than to attempt to move from one part of Scotland to another. Nothing could be more calculated to inhibit personal, social and economic progress. It is particularly damaging in areas of declining industry where movement of the working population is desirable and in some cases vitally necessary. The exchange of council houses, owned by differing local authorities, is also discouraged, and this further restricts movement – particularly of young people.

Many young couples necessarily wish to move house during the first ten years of married life; the present system of council house allocation simply does not cater for their particular requirements and problems. The lists also do not appear to cater for people with large families, for young single men and women, for unmarried mothers or deserted wives, for single or married students and for many other special cases.

Surprising variations occur in the variety of choice given to an applicant who reaches the 'top of the list'. Progressive local authorities offer a reasonable variety of choice and this appears to satisfy most applicants. Some authorities allocate three houses in specific areas, while others simply offer one choice only. Refusal of these 'choices' can mean the withdrawal of an application from the waiting list for anything up to two years. The dark side of some housing lists reveals a grading system for housing applicants, particularly amongst those who do not come up to middle-class standards of behaviour. These unfortunate people are the ones most likely to be given a house in a highly undesirable scheme where facilities are minimal and where maintenance of municipal property is practically non-existent.

There are also considerable variations in the method of updating and maintaining local authority house waiting lists. Some authorities revise the lists 'when necessary' or 'at regular intervals'. With others the period between the updating of lists varies from one to five years. Some lists are partly obsolete, and many do not reflect real housing need in a local area. To make matters worse, the lists form the basis of housing returns which are submitted to the Scottish Development Department to enable this body to make an assessment of the housing problem at national level—which are at best hopelessly unscientific and at worst calculated to 'put a good face' on a bad local situation—have served to fudge national housing requirements and have enabled the central government to conceal the real dimension of Scotland's housing problem for well over fifty years.

Summary

At national level, the promotion, construction, maintenance and general management strategy of housing in the public sector is a highly unsatisfactory and inefficient method of housing people in Scotland. It is a wasteful way of using resources. Many housing specifications are inadequate and many contain 'built-in' maintenance problems. Houses will have to be demolished before the sixty-year repayment period is completed. In some areas empty houses are becoming a social and economic liability to the local authority. Inadequate financial provision for house maintenance purposes ensures that deterioration takes place and that further housing liability will be incurred.

At local level, segregation, lack of choice, paternalistic attitudes, problems of allocation, indifferent methods of housing maintenance and housing management are undesirable features of housing in the public sector. Perhaps these aspects are best summed up in an extract from a recent Shelter report covering Britain, published in 1975, which states:

> The thrust of this report has been that Council tenants are second class citizens. This problem is at its most acute on dump estates, where no-one with any choice will live. Council tenants have no security of tenure; no say in formulating the regulations that govern their tenancy; they frequently have to put up with a completely inadequate repairs and maintenance service, as well as being restricted in the work they are allowed to do to their own house. Some well-off people living on Council estates will object to this analysis and say that they are perfectly happy. This does not alter the fact that Council tenants' status is low in the eyes of the rest of the community.

Shelter makes a plea for tenant control and for the formation of tenant co-operatives, within existing council housing developments. These groups would, they say, be locally based, be managed in small units and would eventually become autonomous. The writer endorses this idea and believes that the imbalance created in favour of council housing in some areas of Scotland – up to 80 per cent of all houses in some areas are owned by local councils – could be moderated by the formation of tenant housing associations or housing co-operatives.

Tenants could be offered a choice of tenure ranging from local self-management associations paying rent to the local authority, to complete group ownership by non-profit-making housing co-operatives. In this way, tenants would have a much greater say in the control, management and day-to-day running of their local communities. Tenants' groups would be responsible for house lettings, for collecting rent and for arranging the day-to-day running of housing in their local areas. They could also organise local labour to carry out maintenance and house repairs.

Glasgow District Council are making a tentative move in the formation of a housing co-operative at Summerston in Glasgow. This is a welcome initiative and must be given every encouragement to ensure success.

I

In 1951, the Conservative Party promised to build a minimum of 300,000 houses a year in Britain (England and Wales). During the period 1951-61, this figure was exceeded once in 1954 when 308,952 houses were completed. The equivalent Scottish figure for that year was 38,653 completions, which was not a particularly impressive figure and certainly not one to excite party political propagandists. The achievement by the Conservatives in England and Wales was loudly proclaimed in Parliament and widely reported in the popular press. This figure compared very favourably with the best performance of the previous Labour administration with 206,405 completions in 1948.

Few people troubled to find out how and why the magic number of 300,000 had been exceeded by the Conservatives. The popular press did little to enlighten them in this; they were concerned to reflect a newsworthy housing statistic and little else. In reality, the record completion figure had been achieved by increasing imports of building materials – something the Labour Party had not dared do during their period as governing party, by increasing housing subsidies to local authorities and, finally, by reducing house sizes and specifications. These reductions were crucial to numerical success. In Scotland, the methods used were roughly similar to those applied in England and Wales, but, unfortunately for the politicians, no magical completion figure could be conjured from the political hat!

The Conservatives reduced house sizes in the following manner: prior to the Second World War the average size of a three-bedroom house in Scotland was 74 sq. metres (800 sq. ft). By 1949, the figure had risen to 84 sq.m (900 sq. ft) and even exceeded 92 sq.m (1,000 sq. ft) in 1951. In 1952 the size of a standard three-bedroom council house had been reduced to 79 sq.m (850 sq. ft). Naturally, little publicity was given to these reduced areas or to the reduction in the quality of building materials used in the 1952-4 housing construction programmes both in Scotland and in Britain as a whole. Numerical achievement had been given priority over all other criteria in British housing policy, simply to boost the credibility of a political party.

Now it might well be asked, what is the significance and relevance of the 1954 record completion figure in the 1970s? In today's terms, it is reasonable to assume that Scotland has inherited 38,653 houses, many of which are undersized and of poor quality; the majority contain 'built-in' defects, which now represent an increasing maintenance and a major cost problem for local authorities. Many of these houses were planned for peripheral city or town sites with indecent haste and without proper thought for layout or for community services. What is more, some of these properties will have to be demolished long before they are finally 'paid off' by tax- and ratepayers in the year 2014. In the long term, it is questionable whether value for money will ever be obtained from many of the houses built during this period.

Priority was thus given to a maximum number of housing completions. This 'British priority' was supported by national and local politicians of all political persuasions in Scotland during the 1950s and 1960s. Numerical obsession still colours the attitudes of many politicians in the 1970s. This problem of priorities crops up again and again in relation to housing in Britain. Professor John Greve sums up the problem of priority neatly when he says:

> Attitudes to housing and thus to housing standards and the priorities by governments and individuals reflect social values as well as the availability of natural resources. A government which arranges economic and social policies in such a way that an exceptionally small proportion of the national product is invested in housing clearly does not place housing very high on its scale of priorities. Such is the case in Britain and has been for many years.

Britain has consistently spent less of her national production on housing than have most countries in Western Europe. This is clearly illustrated in Table 5.1, compiled from recent editions of the *Annual Bulletin of Housing Statistics* for Europe prepared by the United Nations Organisation in Geneva.

From the table certain interesting factors emerge: in 1963, for example, only Southern Ireland spent less of the share of national production on housing than Britain. By 1971, Ireland had surpassed Britain and only Portugal invested less in housing. It should also be noted that 1968 was a record year for housing construction in Britain. By 1971, Ireland increased her share of the national production while Britain's share decreased; Britain still occupies second-bottom position. In 1975, Britain increased her share but cannot match Ireland's greatly increased share of national production. Britain still remains at or near the bottom of the table.

Table 5.1:   Share of the National Production Devoted to House Building
(expressed as a percentage)

	1963	1968	1971	1975
Britain	3.1	3.7	2.9	3.9
Belgium	4.8	5.6	5.1	6.1
West Germany	6.0	5.6	5.9	4.5
Denmark	3.5	4.3	5.0	4.6
Finland	6.3	5.2	6.6	7.0
France	5.4	6.9	6.7	7.3
Ireland	2.8	3.8	4.6	6.2
Italy	6.9	6.3	5.9	6.1
Netherlands	3.8	5.7	5.8	5.2
Norway	4.2	4.8	5.4	5.5
Sweden	5.0	5.3	4.7	4.2
Spain	5.4	3.9	3.3	6.8
Portugal	3.3	2.5	2.5	4.0

In 1970, Britain spent a higher percentage share of her national production on defence (5.7) than any other country in Western Europe with the exception of Portugal, a country which at that time was engaged in waging costly internal wars in her African colonies. The average spent by all NATO countries in 1970 was 4.2. In other words, had Britain been content to spend the NATO average on defence, the net saving would have been somewhere in the region of £600 million pounds. This money, or at least some part of it, might have been chan-nelled into vital rehabilitation and new housing work throughout Britain.

Excessive expenditure on defence highlights a deeply rooted British problem which may be defined as an obsessive concern for international status. The recent pattern of this obsession was firmly established during the 1950s by senior Labour and Conservative politicians, many of whom were steeped in nostalgic political, social and economic beliefs which were popular in the last decades of the nineteenth century. At that time, it could be said that Britain was still the greatest political and economic power on earth. The debilitating effects of two world wars and the econ-omic depression which came between ensured that Britain's major power role was no longer tenable; in spite of this, politicians of all persuasions refused to accept a position of diminished power and influence with good grace and dignity. Even the disastrous escapade at Suez in 1956 could not cure the British government of these illogical and entirely outdated concepts of Britain's place in the community of nations.

The much-vaunted technological revolution engendered by the Wilson administration of the sixties could not, or would not, shake off this obsession with past achievements and glories. No effort was spared to ensure a 'strong £' or to maintain sterling as a reserve currency in the world money markets. The 'independent' and hopelessly expensive nuclear deterrent was also firmly maintained, while a near pathological desire to sit at 'the top table' – any top table – was pursued with elemental vigour.

The Heath administration of the 1970s gave an up-to-date twist to the obsession by continuing to support the absurdly expensive Concorde project, by attempting to designate a third airport round London and by backing the channel tunnel project. The reason given for supporting these projects was, in Mr Heath's own words, 'to maintain our position in the community of nations'.

Lord Rothschild, in a well-reported speech in September 1973, said,

It seems to me that unless we give up the idea that we are one of the wealthiest, most influential countries in the world – in other words that Queen Victoria is still reigning – we are likely to find ourselves in very serious trouble.

He went on to say that Britain could be one of the poorest countries in Europe by 1985, if the country insisted on pursuing this ridiculous and anachronistic posture. Lord Rothschild recognised that our national priorities are hopelessly out of step with reality. This attitude seriously compromises any attempt to run a balanced economy, which in turn seriously affects national housing policies and programmes. The grand obsession in Whitehall and in Westminster ensures that many ordinary people in Scotland cannot hope to be adequately housed or rehoused in the foreseeable future.

II

In a previous chapter, it was noted that available choice in the Scottish housing market was more restricted than in any other Western European country. It was also observed that a greater proportion of state housing (local authority, new towns and government-sponsored housing) is constructed in Scotland than in many Eastern European countries. Quoting again from the *Annual Bulletin of Housing Statistics*, Table 5.2 illustrates the pattern of housing promoter or investor in Europe which emerges.

Table 5.2:   Types of Investor (expressed as percentage)

Country	Investor	1971	1973	1976
Britain	Local authority	42.1	33.0	45.8
	Other public sector	4.3	3.8	5.8
	Private sector	51.7	59.6	47.0
	Private sector aided	1.9	3.6	1.4
Scotland*	Local authority	65.1	48.1	39.4
	Other public sector	15.3	10.5	20.0
	Private sector	19.0	40.7	37.5
	Housing associations	0.6	0.7	3.1
Belgium	Public authorities	0.9	0.9	0.2 (1975)
	Semi-public bodies	0.4	0.1	0.5
	Housing co-ops	3.0	1.3	2.4
	Private bodies	37.6	34.0	32.9
	Private persons	58.1	63.7	64.0
Denmark	State	2.8	0.6	0.9
	Housing associations	27.9	23.3	23.1
	Private persons	64.3	72.1	75.4
	Private persons aided	5.0	4.0	0.6
France	Local authorities	0.6	1.0	0.8 (1974)
	HLM organisation	32.0	23.3	24.7
	Housing corporations	32.7	36.0	35.0
	Private persons	34.7	39.7	39.5
West Germany	Public authorities	2.4	2.0	3.1
	Housing co-ops	17.8	16.7	13.1
	Private sector	56.6	54.0	64.0
	Housing corporations	12.8	15.9	11.4
	Private enterprises	10.4	11.4	8.4
Netherlands	Local authorities	8.9	5.8	4.3 (1975)
	Housing associations	39.6	40.9	33.7
	Private sector	35.7	33.8	40.4
	Private sector aided	15.8	19.5	21.6
Czechoslovakia	State	17.5	22.6	24.6
	Housing enterprises	19.8	21.6	22.0
	Housing co-ops	35.8	29.6	24.0
	Private sector	10.3	17.7	8.0
	Private sector aided	16.6	8.5	21.4
Hungary	State	29.9	32.9	34.5
	Private sector	13.5	12.2	9.9
	Private sector aided	56.6	54.9	55.6
Poland	State	22.7	30.6	20.6
	Housing co-ops	48.9	44.9	56.7
	Private sector	28.4	24.5	22.7
Norway	State	0.4	0.4	0.3 (1975)
	Local authorities	3.5	6.1	4.9
	Housing associations	19.7	24.0	19.1
	Housing enterprises	10.2	13.1	10.8
	Private sector	63.3	53.3	60.8
	Other	2.9	3.1	4.1
Sweden	Local authorities	3.7	1.7	1.7
	Semi-public bodies	42.2	37.9	19.8
	Housing co-ops	14.5	10.1	6.9
	Private sector	39.6	50.3	71.6
Russia	State	71.2	79.4	72.8
	Housing co-ops	6.0	—	—
	Private individuals aided	10.7	9.9	16.6
	Collective farms	12.1	10.7	10.6

*Compiled by the writer.

The table confirms that the principal promoter of housing in Scotland is the state, with the local authority acting as the principal government agent; the lack of variety in the programme is decidedly obvious. This factor directly affects choice in housing and this, in turn, reflects acceptable levels in housing standards. Expectations, values and aspirations are severely restricted by this lack of choice. How can people be expected to develop preferences both in standard and in quality in such restricted circumstances?

Choice in housing has also been restricted in England and Wales, but here at least a more reasonable balance between the public and private sectors has been struck, while the percentage share (not shown on Table 5.2 – approximately 5.4 per cent) of the total production built by housing associations is at least better than the comparable Scottish figure.

Returning to Table 5.2, the percentage spread among the promoters and investors of housing in many European countries is much more evenly distributed than in Scotland. This distribution of promoter and investor is reflected in the standard, quality and variety of houses produced in the various countries. Opportunity is also given for a greater variety of tenure in many European countries; a range of tenure types ranging from owner-occupier to ordinary renting is available to many people in Europe but is largely denied to most people in Scotland.

III

Comparative emphases in house-building programmes between England and Scotland are shown in Tables 5.3 and 5.4, taken from the official housing returns during the period 1950-76. From 1950 until 1953, the main emphasis in both programmes was on local authority housing. By 1954, however, the private market in England and Wales was beginning to catch up with state housing completions, and by 1958 production in the private sector exceeded local authorities by 5 per cent. In the same year, Scottish public sector housing production exceeded production in the private sector by 74 per cent. English and Welsh programmes after 1960 show that the accent on housing production was in the private sector and that a reasonable balance was struck between public and private building programmes. By contrast, the Scottish programme shows consistent emphasis on public sector production throughout the period and an astonishing imbalance between this group and the other housing agencies in Scotland.

The tables also show from 1972 onwards that total housing completions in Scotland began to fall significantly, while annual completions in the private sector rose above 10,000 for the first time since 1919. By

Table 5.3: Extracts from Official Housing Returns (completions) for England and Wales

Year	Local Authority	Housing Associations	Government Depts	Private Builders	New Towns	Total
1950	139,356	1,540	4,888	26,576	—*	172,360
1954	199,642	14,761	6,521	88,028	—	308,952
1958	113,116	1,133	3,159	124,087	—	241,495
1960	103,235	1,650	2,241	162,100	—	269,226
1964	119,468	2,852	3,753	210,432	—	336,505
1968	141,410	6,003	4,401	213,273	6,639	371,726
1970	125,456	8,249	2,059	162,084	9,418	307,266
1972	86,479	7,252	1,785	184,622	7,156	287,294
1973	72,388	8,607	1,738	173,904	6,901	263,538
1974	89,196	9,440	2,684	129,626	10,227	241,173
1975	110,735	13,927	1,529	140,381	12,122	278,694
1976	112,028	14,618	1,413	138,477	12,124	278,660

*Included in the local authority figures until 1968.

Table 5.4: Extracts from Official Housing Returns (completions) for Scotland

Year	Local Authority	New Towns	SSHA	Housing Associations	Govt Depts	Private Builders	Total
1950	20,989	158	3,167	91	624	782	25,811
1954	29,748	1,466	4,117	115	799	2,608	38,853
1958	22,622	1,474	3,277	93	643	4,061	32,170
1960	17,913	1,519	2,071	127	433	6,529	28,592
1964	24,814	2,608	1,734	12	341	7,662	37,171
1968	26,756	3,207	2,048	288	970	8,719	41,988
1970	28,086	2,790	3,525	244	302	8,220	43,167
1972	16,333	1,519	1,739	413	151	11,835	31,990
1973	14,432	1,589	1,328	245	224	12,215	30,033
1974	13,016	2,099	1,067	480	435	11,239	28,336
1975	16,086	3,636	3,062	778	402	10,371	34,335
1976	14,361	3,980	2,813	1,152	517	13,704	36,527

1976, housing completions in the public sector still exceed completions by the other agencies by 18 per cent. Completions by housing associations, though rising slowly, show a consistently low production level, and do not compare favourably with completions by the English housing associations.

IV

During the period from 1919 to 1972, Scottish local authorities amassed an outstanding housing debt of over £1,000,000,000; a great deal of this money is borrowed from private individuals, from large private financial institutions and from international investors in Europe and the Middle East. Subject to government approval, capital expenditure on new housing in Scotland is raised by each local authority from any one of the above sources, or through the offices of the Public Works Loans Board. This institution used to lend money below current market rates, but the practice is now discontinued. The board does, however, aid local authorities which might otherwise have difficulty in raising money through normal financial channels. At this point, it should be noted that the governments of many European countries subsidise the rates of interest charged to housing institutions and organisations who promote the building of houses for lower-paid workers, whereas in Scotland full market rates of interest are imposed on local authorities carrying out similar operations. Some subsidy programmes in Europe enable housing promoters to pay low rates of interest varying between 2 per cent and 4 per cent.

Repayments on money borrowed by local authorities to finance housing programmes are made over a period of 60 years from three main sources: house rents, government subsidy and local rates. This represents local authority income for housing purposes. Expenditure on housing is mainly concerned in servicing the ever-increasing housing debt. Loan charges for all local authorities in Scotland during the period 1972-3 amounted to the staggering total of £106,757,705.

Now provided the principle of usury is accepted as a normal and reasonable method of financing a national housing programme – and this is highly debatable – the housing debt only becomes a burden if houses do not last for 60 years, or if a local authority has insufficient income to offset annual repayments of the housing debt. By way of illustration, Table 5.5 gives a broad analysis of the 1972-3 housing revenue account in Scotland. Under expenditure it is obvious that loan charges on capital borrowed account for 75 per cent of local authority expenditure on housing. This means in money terms that the final cost of an average council house (£8,000 in 1974) paid by the community over 60 years is

Table 5.5: Housing Revenue Account, 1972-3

Expenditure:	%
Loan charges (interest and redemption)	75.50
Repairs to existing housing	17.10
Management costs	7.40
Total	100.00
Income:	
Rents	51.90
Government subsidies	29.50
Rates contributions	17.30
Other income	1.30
Total	100.00

roughly seven times the original bricks and mortar cost, i.e. £56,000.

Under income, the subsidy accounts for approximately 30 per cent of income, and represents the government's sole contribution to the financing of local authority housing. It underlines the low priority given to housing by the exchequer, as mentioned in a previous chapter. Rates are expected to cover approximately 18 per cent of income. This contribution from local rates was initially devised by central government in the early 1920s to enable it to reduce subsidy payments to local authority housing accounts from central funds. This method of financing the housing account has been abused both by central government and by local authorities for many years. It is a grotesquely unfair method of financing local authority house-building programmes in Scotland.

The amount of money raised by rents to finance the housing debt has caused more bitterness, controversy and enmity than any other single issue concerning Scottish housing in the recent past. The issue has intensified social division within communities; it has virtually divided a nation into two camps.

A brief examination of the problem shows that the method of allocating subsidies is different; the council tenant is subsidised by direct government subsidy, whereas the owner-occupier is granted income tax relief on his mortgage payments. The differing methods of subsidy are obviously divisive and liable to cause enmity, in that each group genuinely believes that the system favours the other. Unless a radical change is made in the method of allocating subsidies, the dreary class-ridden arguments are bound to continue. Outdated and outmoded, they are sustained by politicians and local representatives who still eagerly recall the hated means tests of the 1930s, or the 25p per week local authority house of the 1950s. In any sensible analysis of the problem, the need for reform of the subsidy system is undeniable and long overdue. These reforms should include the amount of money granted by central government to housing subsidy, the manner in which this money is raised and a sensible and fair method of allocating the subsidy to all sections of the population.

The Scottish Office estimates that 160,000 dwellings are still below the minimum tolerable standard in Scotland. No figures are available for a substantial number of houses which are just above the tolerance standard, but cannot be regarded as 'tolerable' by modern standards. In 1975 the West Central Scotland Planning Committee estimated that 127,500 pre-1919 houses required immediate improvement or replacement and that two thirds of the 256,000 pre-1919 houses were still lacking in one basic amenity. No figures are available to show the deterioration which has taken place in many local authority pre-war and post-war housing areas. The need for an accurate and all-embracing survey of Scottish housing conditions is vitally necessary and long overdue. The very special nature of Scotland's housing problems cannot clearly be understood or appreciated until this survey is completed and fully analysed. The need for such a survey is underlined by a recent government report: Urban Deprivation Working Note 6, Great Britain, which is based on an analysis of the 1971 national census figures. The report makes depressing reading for those who are concerned with housing problems in Scotland. It confirms what has been suspected for a long time, but never proved, that Scotland contains areas of severe urban deprivation without parallel in the rest of Britain. The figures are impressively clear, as shown in Table 5.6.

Table 5.6: Geographical Distribution of Most Deprived Areas (based on overcrowding, lack of exclusive use of basic amenities and male unemployment)

	England	Scotland	Inner London Boroughs	Clydeside
	%	%	%	%
Share of GB's 5 per cent 'worst areas'	22.4	77.4	3.5	68.1
Share of GB's 1 per cent 'worst areas'	2.5	97.5	1.7	95.0
Population as a percentage of GB population	84.6	11.1	8.6	4.3

Thus, Scotland with only 11.1 per cent of the British population has 77.4 per cent of the 'worst 5 per cent areas' of Britain and a staggering 97.5 per cent of the 'worst 1 per cent areas' of the country. These figures are derived from information on overcrowding, on the lack of exclusive use of all basic amenities in a house and on male unemployment.

Against other conurbations the figures for Clydeside are equally horrific. With 4.3 per cent of the British population, the area accounts for 68.1 per cent of the 'worst 5 per cent areas', and, perhaps the most intense statistic of the whole report, Clydeside represents 95 per cent of the worst 1 per cent of Britain. No other area begins to approach the magnitude of deprivation suffered by Scotland and above all by Clydeside. Using the same combination of measures of deprivation the nearest rival for Clydeside (68.1 per cent) in Britain's 'worst 5 per cent' is the West Midlands of England at a mere 8.1 per cent. The boroughs of Inner London which in other comparisons come a very poor second to Clydeside muster only 3.5 per cent in this respect.

The picture repeats itself with a terrible monotony whatever scale of comparison is chosen. In severe overcrowding Clydeside accounts for 75 per cent of Britain's 'worst 1 per cent' and by comparison London's overcrowded areas, although substantial in number, pale into relative insignificance. The case for special consideration to be given to Scottish housing problems, especially on Clydeside, is unanswerable. The latest round of government 'cuts' in housing expenditure (1975) have already denied the existence of a special problem.

6　HOUSING IN THE PRIVATE SECTOR

I

During the period from 1950 to 1970, annual house completions in the private sector of the English house-building programme were proportionally much higher than corresponding completions in Scotland — reference is made to Tables 5.3 and 5.4. The private sector in Scotland was, and still is, uniquely small (1975), not only when compared with England, but also in comparison to many countries in Western Europe. This low rate of private house building is reflected in the number of owner-occupiers in Scotland, which is in the order of 30 per cent as opposed to 50 per cent in England. Traditionally, many Scots have not regarded themselves as potential owner-occupiers, being content to rely on rented housing in the public sector as the availability of housing in the private rental sector rapidly diminished after the Second World War.

In the twenty-year period until 1970, house building in the Scottish private sector was dominated by a handful of builders; they were responsible for approximately 75 per cent of all housing completions in this sector. In 1968, the largest private house builder produced 25 per cent of the total Scottish output; this compared with a figure of 5 per cent for the largest house builder in England during the same period. The supply of new houses in most areas of Scotland was kept below, or even well below, demand level; this ensured a continuing seller's market — a seller's market in private housing existed more or less continuously from 1950 to 1970 in Scotland. The supply of land for building houses was also restricted because large areas of prime house-building land in and around the principal cities of Scotland were owned by a small number of house builders. Private house builders, while favouring large housing developments, were inclined to develop sites over a lengthy period of time, by building between 30 and 50 houses per annum on a site with a final development figure of some 500 houses.

An interesting and contrasting situation occurred in Yorkshire during the same period: here, a much more open and flexible situation gave opportunities for a range of medium and small builders to construct houses on a variety of sites, many of which were quite small in area — between 5 and 10 acres. Few, if any, of these builders owned large plots of land, while many appeared to buy ground immediately prior to the commencement of building operations. This contrast, both in attitude

96

and approach, seemed to reflect in house prices; according to Professor
Sidwell in his recent report for the Scottish Housing Advisory Committee
(1969), the price of an average two-storey, three-bedroom house in Yorkshire (1969) was approximately £1,000 cheaper than the equivalent
house in the Central Lowland areas of Scotland at a time when the cost
of building land was dearer in Yorkshire than in central Scotland.

While it is admitted in the report that additional costs for Scottish
house construction could be attributed to the higher standards set by
building and water regulations, to the severity of the Scottish climate,
to shorter working hours in winter and to higher earnings of Scottish
building operatives, Sidwell believed that the area of accountability for
the price differentiation between Yorkshire and Scotland was caused by
two other factors, namely productivity and profit. He might also have
emphasised the lack of demand for a low-cost house in the private sector
of the market in Scotland.

From 1950 until 1970, little attempt was made by private house
builders in Scotland to improve house design or housing layout plans;
there was little incentive for them to change anything. One builder even
boasted that there was no reason for change or improvement in a situation which was so completely favourable to his company. Unfortunately,
this typified an attitude which ensured that little progress in housing
design could be made and that the period-piece offerings of the 1930s,
modified somewhat to suit conditions of the early 1950s, would continue to dominate the private sector in Scotland long after the end of the
Second World War. In defence of this hopelessly unimaginative and rep-
rehensible attitude, the house builder maintains that he is 'giving the
public what it wants' and that he cannot afford to experiment, to try new
ideas, or to take any risks. He argues that the general public in Scotland
is unwilling to try new ideas or to take any risks when buying a new
house.

House purchasers in Scotland—and this includes purchasers in the
top price range of the private housing market—are very undemanding in
their requirements; they set few standards. In domestic terms, design
appreciation is strictly limited, attitudes to housing design hopelessly
conservative. The dreadful paltriness of the average suburban street also
excites little critical response. The harsh aridity of wide 'landing strip'
approach roads, grotesque concrete 'art-form' lamp standards, inadequate
landscaping, race-track roadway systems, the general lack of common
space, play space or accidental meeting space are all accepted as a normal
and natural backcloth to suburban living in Scotland. The proper organisation of the approach space to housing both for pedestrians and for

vehicles – the vital transitional area between the public and the private domain – is scarcely considered. Public zones and private zones within houses at ground-floor level are hopelessly mixed; privacy is at a premium in the average private housing layout in Scotland.

The problem of orientation in housing also receives little consideration. Many housing layouts tend to favour a dining/living plan at ground floor level with large windows to front and back elevation; this 'through plan' form of layout can be adopted to suit most building sites, but does little to solve the problem of room orientation. Situations arise where the kitchen of a house has ample sunlight, while the kitchen of an identical house on the opposite side of the road obtains little or no sunlight at all. In this type of layout, the living room is always positioned to the front, i.e. to the side of the house facing the street, regardless of orientation. Privacy is hopefully obtained by a traditional though often much foreshortened semi-public garden entrance way while privacy at the back of the house is simply determined by the minimal distance between houses permitted by the building regulations.

Indifferent internal planning and poor spacial relationships, bad kitchen layouts, impossibly small bedrooms, inadequate storage arrangements, lack of facilities for study and for hobbies, no provision for adaption or extension and poor garaging or car parking facilities receive little critical appraisal. Inadequate wall and roof insulation, poor window design and poor internal and external finishes cause little or no comment. Few prospective house buyers appreciate that most public sector housing plans actually provide better-proportioned spaces, slightly larger rooms, better-designed kitchens and more storage accommodation than the equivalent house displayed in glossy sales literature.

Critical interest in housing design and housing layout occurs at a remarkably superficial level; considerable interest is taken in kitchen fittings, although the layout for these items may be very badly planned. A coloured bathroom suite, surrounded by a few cheap ceramic tiles, however badly positioned, always makes a good impression. Enthusiasm for imitation stonework, plastic shutters, for 'old worlde' bull's eye windows. wrought iron lamps and other external trivia, all denote a poverty of understanding on the part of prospective buyers. The value of good design in housing is not appreciated and is certainly not understood by many.

II

Our first priority is to find out what people want and are prepared to pay for. Here we take advantage of the range of market research, from

the maximizing of our personal knowledge of our customers to direct
structured interviews of the 'gallup poll' type.

This statement, made by a managing director of a house-building and
contracting firm which is based in the south-east of England, provides
an interesting, though not necessarily typical, contrast to current attitudes
adopted by house builders in Scotland. Here, the use of market research
techniques is considered to be 'a waste of time'; it is also widely believed
that hunch and experience more than equal the scientific approach to
consumer requirements in housing.

The director goes on to say:

Having determined the ceiling price which people are prepared to pay
for a product, how can we best spend the money? Here we work
openly and constructively with architects, both within the company
and also with many outside firms, reconciling the problems of profitability, saleability and buildability in order to set up design and
cost criteria.

The contrasting situation in Scotland is very different.

At a recent forum on private housing, attended by builders, architects
and planners, two of the speakers—house builders—questioned the
architects' ability to assist them with housing development. They emphasised that 'better design costs too much' and that practising architects in
Scotland 'do not have their feet on the ground'. It may well be argued
that builders have their feet so firmly planted into the ground that no
movement or progress is possible. From the tone of the discourse it was
obvious that a polarity of opinion exists between architects and builders
which cannot be allowed to continue indefinitely; the traditional arms'-
length architect/builder relationship is a shameful reflection on the in-
ability of each party to see the other's point of view. It must be hoped
that the hard-line attitude of those vociferous speakers at the forum is
not entirely representative of all house builders in Scotland.

At the same meeting, a planner made a plea for greater co-operation
between builders and the planning departments of local authorities.
Examples were shown of housing developments which were considered
of an acceptable standard. But here again a polarity appeared to exist
between each group. Builders are extremely sensitive to the delays and
restrictions imposed on them by local planning departments, by highway
authorities and other public utility services. It was recently estimated
that delays add a minimum of 5 per cent to the cost of an average house.

In theory, planning permission for a housing development should take
two months; it may in fact take 18 months or even longer. Builders are
also concerned about differing and often opposing standards set by
planners and by the highways and service departments. Differing opinions
here can lead to much confusion and frustration.

Under present conditions, a house builder who wishes to obtain highway and public services approval with the least possible delay is well
advised to submit a standardised stereotyped housing layout to the
authorities. By doing this he can avoid the problem of dealing with
strait-jacket highway control restrictions, problems with local services,
fire, ambulance services, etc. In addition, the stereotyped planning layout has the advantage of allowing the builder to off-load all responsibility
for the public spaces in his development on to the local authority and
all responsibility for private spaces on to each house purchaser. More will
be said about this important aspect of housing layout in the next chapter.

A planning officer can hardly refuse an application for a standard layout on aesthetic grounds, unless he has the positive backing of his planning committee, or unless a proposed development is situated in a place
with obvious vernacular character, or in a designated conservation area.
He can, however, 'tinker' with house-planning layouts, and with the
general appearance of the development; he can also alter densities,
request additional car-parking spaces and possibly add a few kinks to
the access roads. The end result will be little better than the original
builder's submission, but the delay caused by these adjustments can
cause frustration and even financial hardship to the builder which should
not be minimised—least of all by planners.

On the positive side, a good planning officer can make significant
improvements to a builder's housing layout, provided he indicates his
requirements at an early stage. He can also obtain reasonable density,
good open spaces and play spaces and adequate footpaths by dint of
sheer personality and can, in the case of a large development, ensure that
adequate provision is made for community services.

III

Since 1970, a number of house builders from England have opened
branch offices in Scotland and this has led to a greater choice within
the very limited range of standard house plans and layouts. It would
appear that the gap in price range between Scotland and the north of
England has narrowed, though this is not entirely due to the increased
presence of English builders in the country. Production in the private
sector is slowly rising: this is noted in Table 5.5.

Some firms, particularly those who are building in the medium and high price ranges, have attempted to improve their house designs and layouts with limited success, but these developments are few in number. In the low price range—now £14,000—little improvement can be observed. Standard layout plans are still very much in evidence; these are being applied with equal insensitivity to city, town and village all over the country. Varying site conditions still make little difference to the average house builder in Scotland; superb sites are still being wrecked by the mindless application of standard house plans.

This price range constitutes approximately 80 per cent of the private housing market in Scotland and it is here that the builder, the architect and planner must co-operate to improve the general standard of the domestic environment across the country. In what way can architects and planners help the builder to produce a better product? An examination of typical builder-work costs in Scotland gives the following elemental break-down which is expressed as a percentage:

Foundations	5.00
Walls	19.50
Roof	1.50
Internal joinerwork	11.00
Kitchen units	1.00
Sanitary fittings	1.00
Internal finishings	13.00
Heating	4.50
External decoration and landscaping	2.50
Garage	2.00
Access roads	6.00
Public services	2.50
Cost of land (varies between 5% and 20%)	6.00
Sales cost	2.00
Solicitors' fees	0.50
Builder's profit (includes overheads, maintenance, loan interest charges and income tax)	22.00
Total	100.00

Given this break-down of costs as a guide, it is difficult to see where the architect could make savings to the actual fabric of a house; under present circumstances this would be highly undesirable. In the case of land costs—which in some situations might be as high as 20 per cent of total house costs—the architect can certainly help to make economies by increasing density without consequent loss of amenity; he can also render valuable assistance on difficult or non-standard sites. He could also help to design sensible access roads, which would be more appropriate for domestic developments—the provision of a by-law access road and public services presently accounts for 8.5 per cent of the total builder-work cost. The general appearance of private housing developments could be improved, with possible cost savings, provided 'new town' design standards were applied. This does not imply slavish imitation of existing housing designs in new towns. Finally, the architect could help to produce designs which can readily be altered or extended both in terms of additional living space or garaging accommodation.

Planners could assist builders by giving clear and concise indications of what constitutes acceptable domestic development in their area. If necessary, a design guide booklet should be published on the subject. Some initiative must be taken by Scottish planners to break the highway/ public services strait-jacket, which is responsible for the indifferent appearance of so many new housing developments in Scotland. In this respect, the Essex County Council (now defunct) published a design guide which pointed the way to a more enlightened and flexible approach to the design of access roads and public service layouts. The new regions in Scotland should consider the production of a similar document which could be applied to local Scottish conditions.

The builder must also do something towards the creation of a better domestic environment. He might be persuaded to reduce his own profit margin provided land costs, solicitors' and estate agents' fees, sales over-heads and interest rates could also be reduced. He could also lobby local authorities to allow a prospective buyer to install his own kitchen units and to provide most of the internal finishings on his own initiative. Provision could also be made for central heating to be installed at a later date. Savings made by any of these methods should be passed on to the consumer.

The builder also has a moral obligation to act in a socially responsible manner—he can and should no longer expect to plan outdated standard house types, on any site, in any part of the country, or to provide in-flexible, badly designed housing with impunity. It is perhaps ironic that some of the best housing designs in the public sector—bearing in mind the added frustration of dealing with the bureaucracy and cost restrict-ions of government agencies—are still superior to comparable house des-igns produced by the private sector in Scotland.

7 ARCHITECTS, PLANNERS AND BUILDERS

I

'If houses are badly designed – and there are good and bad schemes – it is surely not our fault but the architects'.' This statement is quoted from a recent interview given by a former Minister of Housing to the magazine *Building Design* and represents a predictable official reaction to current problems in housing design. The Minister is expressing a point of view which has some justification – there are many depressingly badly designed housing schemes in existence. Nevertheless, his statement deliberately over-simplifies a complex problem and the former Minister knows this very well.

Perhaps his successors should seriously consider one major aspect of housing design which causes a great deal of confusion and frustration, and is arguably one of the main reasons for poor design performance by official and consultant architects who work in the public housing sector. Housing design in this sector is subjected to a mind-bending series of controls, checks and constraints both at local and national level. Here is a summary of the checkpoints confronting the housing designer in the public sector:

Control, Check, Constraint – Local Level

Land purchase:	often long, arduous and cumbersome – permissions required at both local and national levels.
District valuer control: (official local valuer of land)	delays caused by under-staffed offices which appear to be permanently in this condition.
Provision of services:	holds the key to housing development in many areas.
Local legal control:	can cause considerable delay.
Local council approval control:	mentioned at length in Chapter 4.
Local building by-law control:	difficult to understand and becoming more and more restrictive – must be revised.
Local planning control:	often too restrictive – ironically sometimes not restrictive enough.

Control, Check, Constraint — Local Level

Local highway control:	highly restrictive and environmentally disastrous.
Local public services control:	should be straightforward but can depend on local controllers.
Local cost control:	duplicated at national level — see below.
Other local controls:	small by comparison with other controls — can create delays and problems.
Constraints by local residents:	probably one of the few entirely justifiable controls.

Control, Check, Constraint — National Level

Treasury control:	remote, arbitrary and highly secretive.
Administrative control:	theoretical, bureaucratic and cumbersome.
Strait-jacket cost control:	imposed by the Treasury with the aid of the Scottish Development Department.
Cost ratio problem control:	mentioned later in Chapter 8.
Technical control:	often concerned with petty problem of detail — used as a delaying tactic.
Delaying tactics control:	one of the most frustrating and useless controls — quoted at length in Chapter 4.

To this formidable list must be added a time-scale and a 'frustration' factor. In a previous chapter, it was suggested that the average time taken to obtain all permissions to build might be five years or more, while the actual contract building period could vary between 18 months and two years. Few architects have the will-power, or indeed the staying power, to complete even part of the obstacle course described above. Creativity, dedication, enthusiasm and genuine involvement are difficult, if not impossible, to sustain under such trying circumstances. Many 'give up' by ceasing to function as creative people, reluctantly inhabiting a paper-passing dream world which is the day-to-day reality of public sector housing. Some seek the dubious consolations of promotion and increased salaries — in many local authorities and large private architectural offices, the substitution of a desk for a drawing board is regarded by many as a sign of advancement. Others, hopefully, seek a difference 'course' or a different part of the 'course' in new surroundings. The 'checkpoint' game, however, remains the same! The frustration factor occurs at all stages in the course. Caused mainly by petty power struggles between departments at local level, and the not so petty struggles at national level, it is fuelled by the dark frustration of the obstacle course and by the certain knowledge that the pinstriped hatchet man is waiting — not far away.

At this point, it should be noted that the clients (the people for whom the houses are designed) are hardly considered and certainly never consulted during any stage in the course.

It would be impossible and probably undesirable to describe the problems created by the checkpoint system in great detail. Some of its more disturbing features have been described in previous chapters. A few more are now given below.

The first problem is concerned with land designation. Theoretically, land considered suitable for house building is proposed to a local council by a planning officer, is sanctioned by it and is then ratified by the Development Department in Edinburgh. An 'appropriate' housing density is also fixed and agreed. Some of these sites, particularly in the industrial areas of Scotland, are most unsuitable for housing development — most private housing developers would refuse to build on them — both in terms of size and in relationship to surrounding development. When a car-parking ratio, a density factor and a regulated roadway pattern are added to the equation, the task of creating a decent domestic environment becomes exceedingly difficult.

The Scottish Building Standards Regulations are written in a curious, semi-legalistic style which baffles the simple-minded and the not so simple-minded alike. People at all levels in the building industry have expressed misgivings about the existing format, which is constantly being updated, but does not seem to become easier to understand. Incomprehensibility is not the only problem: housing legislation in Scotland is more restrictive than in England. Some aspects of convenience, which in England have been left to the discretion of the local planning authority, form an integral part of the Building Regulations in Scotland; these include daylighting standards, distance between living-room windows, a maximum walk up a distance of three flights of stairs, internal and external fire-access requirements for three-storey housing, and so on. The restrictive nature of these regulations ensures that innovation, flexibility and creativity in house design and layout can only be frustrated. It is now impossible to embody some of the best traditional features of Victorian and Georgian housing into contemporary housing designs without breaking the building regulations. Priority must be given to a re-

appraisal and revision of the existing regulations to allow for more flexibility and variety in housing design.

Another important area where constraints and controls have had a
disastrous environmental effect is concerned with roads and highway
control. Not only does this constraint throw a strait-jacket round housing
design, it is also most wasteful in terms of land use and resources. It has
been estimated that between 30 per cent and 50 per cent of land associated with new housing development is taken up by roads, pavements
and areas of ground concerned with regulation traffic, turning circles
and sight lines at road junctions. Leslie Ginsburgh, writing in the *Architectural Review* of October 1973, says,

> the main feature of so much of our housing today is paradoxically
> not the housing. It is the unnecessary tarmac—as if every road was
> designed for two pantechnicons to pass at high speed—and spaces
> left over after planning at every roadside, corner, junction or odd bit
> of land.

This tarmac wilderness area is also wasteful both in terms of capital and
of resources. Under present conditions, highway engineers are able to
impose first-class finishing standards to roads serving houses which are
mostly finished to third-class standards in terms of materials. The highway
regulations for local access roads must be seriously and constructively
reconsidered. Much more flexibility is desirable, particularly where local
conditions demand alternative solutions. Access roads in residential areas
should be considered as pedestrian areas into which the motorist is allowed as a privilege and not as a right!

Apart from the formidable problem of meeting and complying with
the indicative costs for housing as laid down by the Treasury, there are
a number of other factors which have to be taken into consideration
before building approval can be assured. These cost factors vary with
current administrative and political policies and relate mainly to aspects
of density. Theoretically, the indicative cost is a closed system based on
standards, cost and density in which density is the only variable; in practice, however, density is often determined by the indicative cost and not
by local social or planning criteria. For example, a local authority may
wish to build a certain number of a particular type of house on a given
site. If the number and type do not 'balance out' in accordance with the
theoretical economic cost of the site, then changes have to be made to
make the site 'balance' regardless of local needs and requirements.

There are instances, particularly in existing urban areas, where local authorities have a special obligation to build new housing in an appropriate style to comply with traditional housing layouts; in this respect, a special cost allowance would be most advantageous and highly desirable. In many cases, special allowances are not made available and cannot be made available due to strait-jacket indicative cost controls and, ultimately, to the inflexibility of remote Treasury control. Examples of this extremely narrow-minded and short-sighted policy can be seen in the older parts of most Scottish burghs and cities.

Lord Goodman, a former chairman of the Housing Corporation, said, amongst other things, that housing problems in Britain must be tackled with passion. Two kinds of passion are possible when confronted by the stupefying bureaucratic systems now imposed. These are frustration and anger. Most professionals cannot afford, or believe they cannot afford, the luxury of the latter. The former is therefore the norm and it is highly debilitating. There is now little or no room for the architect to manoeuvre. As far as the public sector is concerned—and here again, it is emphasised, this sector constitutes the bulk of all new Scottish housing—bureaucracy and mediocrity have won the day.

There is little in recent public sector housing which may be recognised as pleasing domestic architecture. There is no discernible tradition and certainly little attempt to create a satisfying urban backcloth for people in Scotland. There are, of course, some developments of distinction and quality—but these are few and far between and appear to be accidental, almost special cases, instead of the desirable norm. In every case, some-one with more than average design ability made an effort to bend the bureaucratic strait-jacket—just a little—so that he or she could make a satisfactory contribution to contemporary domestic architecture. Under present conditions the problem faced by an architect who is interested or feels committed to housing design in Scotland is possibly best sum-med up by a recent quote of a visiting American architect, who said, 'It's all screwed up here, baby—better leave before they screw you too!'

II

Traditionally, the building industry in Scotland suffers from under-capitalisation, is dependent on substantial bank overdrafts and on the accommodating forbearance by suppliers of building materials to main-tain solvency. The industry still relies on a pool of casual labour, both skilled and unskilled, to man construction projects—a situation which is hardly conducive to good working relationships, or to continuity of employment.

Continuity of operations is something the industry has always lacked;

it is particularly susceptible to national trade recessions. Post-war governments in Britain have developed a nasty habit of using the industry as an economic regulator for the economy of the country as a whole. As the principal employer of the construction industry in Scotland, the government has been able to restrict public sector building projects with indecent haste during a time of 'economic cooling off'.

Needless to say, this tactic restricts investment, leads to bankruptcy, causes instability and a general lack of continuity within the building industry. House building forms a substantial part of government-sponsored construction work in Scotland and is obviously highly susceptible to 'economic regulator control'. For this reason and because of lengthy bureaucratic and highly restrictive processes, local authority housing contracts are not particularly attractive to the building industry. Building houses for local authorities is one of the industry's less popular activities. Many building firms are reluctant to tender for housing contracts and some refuse to submit prices for housing projects as a matter of principle. Competitive tendering for public housing developments by a 'fixed price contract' is highly unpopular with many contractors, who argue – rightly or wrongly – that the 'indicative cost system' tied to a 'fixed price' – particularly during a time of rising inflation – allows for very low profit margins and may, in certain circumstances, result in no profit at all!

The building industry in Scotland is divided roughly into three main work groups which are: large, medium and small contractors. Many of the large building firms are now directed by persons who have little or no site experience, who know next to nothing about building construction and who have little feeling for, or sense of involvement with, the actual business of building. They act purely as financial controllers to the company and to its shareholders. This emphasis is also, unfortunately, reflected in middle management, which tends to be more cost control than site control orientated in outlook. Not surprisingly, bad workmanship on site excites little comment from the management of these firms. It is expected, tolerated, even sometimes condoned by large contracting firms; this is especially true in the case of housing contracts where standards in general are of a very low order. Architects may sometimes be forgiven for believing that they are acting as the contractors' unpaid quality controller on many public housing contracts.

Building tradesmen are themselves caught up in this negative attitude to quality control; they are also subjected to the monotony of highly repetitive work on large housing contracts which requires little thought and the minimum of skills. In such unfavourable circumstances, pride in

workmanship and job satisfaction can have little meaning for a con-
scientious tradesman. Extra money gained from erecting x number of
units in y number of hours under a soulless bonus payment system is
small compensation for a complete loss of job satisfaction which occurs
on many large building contracts. The writer believes that many tradesmen would agree, but would be reluctant to express this point of view
openly for fear of ridicule by their workmates.

Some medium-sized building firms suffer from the same financial bias
at upper- and middle-management levels; small firms do not in general
have this problem: ironically, many of them will have to become more
cost-conscious to maintain solvency in the near future. Both groups contain firms which are also indifferent to quality control and to maintaining standards of good workmanship – the large building organisations
most certainly do not have a monopoly of these particular problems.
There are a number of medium and small builders, however, who consistently produce good standards and who give the impression of caring
about the finished product. Their numbers are decreasing as the century
progresses.

Following from this brief summary of the building industry in Scotland, it is suggested that too many building contracts, especially housing
contracts, are too large, thus necessitating and encouraging the development of large contracting organisations. With one or two notable exceptions, most large contemporary buildings or groups of buildings are inhuman and irrelevant to ordinary human needs and aspirations; they are
boring to design, to detail, to cost and to build. On completion, many
of these buildings diminish the environment, both oppressing and depressing those who come in contact with them.

III

The building trade unions in Scandinavia and also in parts of Europe
play a significant and positive part in the house-building industry. The
scale and extent of their operations, particularly in Sweden and Germany,
were discussed in Chapters 2 and 3.

Here in Scotland, the building trade unions show little interest or
desire to promote and to manage builder-work operations. They are content to follow a traditional and somewhat limited role of securing
employment, wage standards and conditions for their members. In common with the Scottish trade union movement as a whole, the building
unions support the idea that housing is a social service and appear to
accept that the responsibility for the promotion and management of
'social housing' lies exclusively with local authorities. Superficially, this

seems reasonable. Examined more closely, however, it does seem strange that the unions have accepted a concept of housing promotion and management which is basically similar to the private landlord/tenant relationship of the nineteenth century. As stated previously, tenants of local authority houses lack security of tenure, are subjected to one-sided conditions of tenancy, paternalistic attitudes of local officialdom, indifferent management and repair services, have little choice in the selection of position or type of accommodation and cannot move easily from one local authority house to another.

Local authorities may also be controlled by political groups who are unsympathetic to the idea of building social housing for the lower-paid workers. These groups might be in control of a local authority for many years and, provided they enjoy the continued support of the local electorate, there is very little local unions can do to ensure that adequate social housing provision is made for working people in particular districts.

It is also difficult to understand why the idea of local worker control in the building industry has largely been discounted by the building unions in Scotland. This attitude may stem from government indifference and lack of support; it may also be due to a lack of enthusiastic and positive backing from the retail co-operative movement in Scotland. Similar organisations gave considerable moral and financial support to union-sponsored building activities in Scandinavia. It is also suggested that tradesmen in Scotland may not be ready to shoulder the responsibility and discipline required to run a successful worker-controlled building group.

There are a number of worker-controlled building organisations which operate successfully and competitively with private building firms in the midlands of England. These groups are sponsored by the retail co-operative societies and enjoy the support of the local building unions. Operating costs compare very favourably with those quoted for comparable organisations run by private enterprise.

The building unions in Scotland could also act positively in this respect, although not necessarily in the same manner; in the first place they could form study groups to examine the extent and nature of any projected management and control involvement with house-building operations. Progressive worker-controlled building groups in Europe and Scandinavia have shown considerable initiative in this respect by employing architects, planners, administrative and management experts to advise them on technical and financial matters; they have bought land from discerning local authorities and have also competed successfully on the open tendering market for housing contracts. These organisations have helped greatly to improve design, to raise housing standards; they also spend money on research and development and monitor national house-building costs. The Scottish building unions could also, by study, advocacy and example, contribute to the improvement of general living standards in Scotland.

IV

The activities of planners and architect-planners have been subjected to a great deal of criticism in the recent past. Much of the adverse comment is unfortunately relevant and justifiable, particularly in respect of housing. Before making further comments on this thorny issue, it is necessary to give a brief résumé of some of the events which have influenced the thinking behind recent house-planning concepts in Scotland.

In 1918, the Tudor Walter Committee, set up by the government to examine problems especially related to housing, recommended, amongst other things, a drastic reduction in housing density, lavish provision for access roads and a standard distance between houses to ensure adequate sunlight and daylighting. Inspired, no doubt, by the pioneering work of Ebenezer Howard at Letchworth Garden City in England, the committee's recommendations were based on a desire to avoid the worst excesses of speculative housing built for lower-paid workers before the First World War. These recommendations were adopted by the government of the day and now form the basis of a planning code which inhibits progressive housing design. Numerous additions have been made to the code, especially in response to the substantial planning legislation enacted at the end of the Second World War. Aspects of the restrictive nature of the code have already been discussed in this chapter and also in Chapter 6.

In 1937, the Barlow Commission was set up to study the distribution of the industrial population in Britain as a whole. The commission reported in 1940, suggesting amongst other things that a central authority be established to facilitate the redevelopment of congested urban areas and to disperse industries and industrial population accordingly. To carry out this operation, the commission proposed the creation of satellite towns, trading estates and the planned redevelopment of existing small towns or regional centres.

At the end of the war, the government generally supported these proposals. In October 1945, it set up a New Towns Committee under the chairmanship of Lord Reith

'to consider the general question of the establishment, development,

organisation and administration that will arise in the promotion of
New Towns in furtherance of a policy of planned decentralisation
from congested urban areas; and in accordance therewith to suggest
guiding principles on which towns should be established and developed as self-contained and balanced communities for work and living.'

In 1946, the New Towns Act was passed. The adoption of the policy
marked the summation of many thoughts on town-planning problems;
these were concerned with disorder, congestion, dirt, slums and overcrowding. There was a desire to direct urban growth and to replace
aimless shifts of population with constructive policies. There was concern over the loss of fertile agricultural soil for housing, commercial and
industrial development; there was also discontent with the monotonous
housing built before the war, with housing unrelated to employment
centres or community facilities; and there was an impatience with the
single-minded trading estate policy which encouraged industries in de-
pressed economic areas, but overlooked housing and community facilities and also industrial development in other areas.

Under the terms of the new legislation, both local and national
policy was to decide the essential character of a community in advance.
Private decisions were to be made within the framework of an over-all
plan which embodied social goals. Development in the urban areas was
no longer to be an accidental by-product of countless individual decisions made for the benefit of private profit.

Understandably, planners were inspired by the New Towns Act and
other relevant legislation, which enabled local authorities to set up
local planning controls. Statements from the Barlow Report concluding
that rapid industrialisation in the nineteenth century had led to 'disastrous harvests of slums, sickness, stunted population and human
misery' no doubt acted as a spur for planners to cope with the legacy
of bad housing in Scotland. Planners were given further incentive by
the rapid growth of private transport during the 1950s, which seemed
to render existing road patterns obsolete in a very short space of time.

To meet these demands, plans were prepared for the existing urban
areas, which presupposed finite solutions to planning problems. These
plans denied the simple principle of urban dynamics which demonstrates
that urban growth starts with an empty land area, develops a life cycle
leading to full land occupancy and to equilibrium. Unless there is continuing renewal and a genuine appreciation of the existence of this
process, then 'growth and development' and 'equilibrium' will be followed by 'stagnation' and, finally, a 'decay' situation will complete the

cycle in any given urban area.

At the end of the Second World War, many housing areas in urban Scotland had already reached a state of 'stagnation'. In the west of Scotland and also on Tayside, the planners' concept of 'a brave new world' approach to urban housing problems coincided with the local politicians' idea of an intensive programme of municipal house building. As a result of this unholy alliance, existing housing areas in 'stagnation' became areas in 'decay' by official default; demolition completed the process with sickening finality. In the areas most affected by this crude manipulation and acceleration of the cycle, complex urban living patterns, interweaving and interacting over wide areas and across many imagined boundaries, were unwittingly destroyed. The 'new world' concept had accelerated out of control, as many citizens who were unfortunate enough to live in an affected area found to their cost.

It is now being reluctantly appreciated that 'growth and development' in the form of redevelopment should take place shortly after demolition is completed, otherwise a pattern of 'decay' spreads quickly to surrounding areas. It is difficult to imagine that this operation can be carried out successfully by a country which is in a constant state of economic crisis or near-economic crisis and gives low priority to housing and to housing redevelopment. It is also clear that the bureaucratic processes which presently 'direct' these operations, both at local and national level, are incapable of making a careful transition between demolition and redevelopment. Scotland simply cannot afford to carry out large-scale housing redevelopment under present-day conditions.

Planners must therefore learn to content themselves with a much more careful and sensitive approach to urban housing problems; they have to learn that demolition is a last resort and that housing in the 'stagnation' stage of development can be brought back to a state of 'equilibrium' with less effort than might be supposed. Planning for 'equilibrium' shows sensitivity to all existing urban communities, is mindful of the past, understands the present and looks wisely to the future. Redevelopment is effected with the minimum of demolition; new buildings are inserted into the existing fabric with the care and precision of a watchmaker.

Consultation with local people was unfashionable in the 'heroic' period of many urban redevelopment programmes. It is now appreciated, if somewhat reluctantly, that people must be allowed to participate – to have a say in the redevelopment process. People understand the working of their own districts with surprising clarity; they also cherish – often unwittingly – the cluttered disorganisation which forms a backcloth to their everyday lives. Planners really must leave their comfortable offices, throw away many of their maps, models and diagrams and move out to small local district offices. Here they would gain an understanding and appreciation of a local area and how it is used by local people. They would be acting as advisers to a local community and not as remote manipulators of an official policy. Localised planners would soon become known to and, hopefully, respected by local people; their advice would be sought and, on occasion, taken which, in the writer's opinion, is as it should be. This concept of a localised planning role presupposes the development of strong community councils to direct or to take advice from local planners. People everywhere, and this applies even to the new towns, must not miss this opportunity to take vital decisions affecting their daily lives.

V

Little has so far been said about Scotland's new towns and, more particularly, about the housing in these communities. There are five new towns in Scotland: East Kilbride (designated 1947), Glenrothes (1948), Cumbernauld (1955), Livingstone (1962), and Irvine (1966). Initially, the new towns had projected populations of between 35,000 and 60,000 people. Following in the garden-city tradition and to meet a demand for houses with gardens, the first new housing areas were planned at very low densities. To counter adverse criticism of this policy and in an attempt to achieve a more urban environment, densities were increased and the over-all population levels were raised; e.g., the initial population target for East Kilbride was 50,000; this was first increased to 70,000 and finally to 100,000 people.

A considerable administrative problem has been experienced by the new-town development corporations who are largely responsible for the new housing construction in the new towns. Differences of opinion between the new-town corporations and adjoining local authorities have caused delays to housing programmes. The problem of attempting to design and build 500-1,000 houses to a satisfactory standard and to meet 'political' deadlines should not be minimised.

The ideal of a varied and balanced housing development within the new towns has been constantly upset by inconsistent government policies, with problems caused by long- and short-term cost allocations and a general lack of investment in housing development from all sources. In many cases, private capital was discouraged from making a contribution to the new housing programmes.

Originally, it was intended that new-town inhabitants should live and work within the boundaries of a new-town area and that they should form a 'balanced community' of people drawn as far as possible from all groups in society. Attempts to achieve this balance have been unsuccessful in so far as most inhabitants in the new towns come from skilled and semi-skilled working groups. Few professional, administrative and managerial workers have been attracted to the new towns. This may be due to the type of housing tenure offered in the new towns – the vast majority of houses are rented from the local development corporation. This is consistent with the pattern of public sector tenure in Scotland and also underlines the lack of choice offered to the population as a whole. Increasing emphasis is now being placed on owner-occupation and this may help to redress the lack of balance within these communities. The provision of homes for owner-occupation may not be of much assistance to unskilled workers, who have been discouraged from renting houses within the new towns for various 'official' reasons.

Critics have complained that the new towns are little better than commuter suburbs, that little or no provision is made for shopping and community services, particularly in the early stages of new-town development, that many neighbourhood areas look like vast council housing schemes and that many people, especially housewives, suffer from mental disorders or even just 'new town blues'. It has also been said that the new towns suffer from a lack of warmth, sensual delight, surprise, stimulus and drama and that little provision has been made for young people or for old people in these colourless, television-orientated noddy-lands. The writer was particularly disappointed to see so many badly finished houses and to note a general lack of maintenance throughout many of the new-town housing areas. It was also depressing to see so much litter and rubbish lying about in many public spaces. When will Scots in general start caring about their domestic surroundings?

In spite of these and other criticisms, many people have gained by coming to live in the new communities. Each new town has in turn gained a reputation for producing housing layouts and designs which are generally of a higher standard than those produced by local authorities and private builders in Scotland. Some of the housing layouts produced by the new-town corporations may well be regarded in later years as the best examples of housing development carried out in Scotland during the post-war period.

Housing societies and associations carry on the business of constructing and managing house property. They are organised on a non-profit-making basis for the benefit of members who rent or have a share in houses under the terms of a tenancy agreement or lease granted to them by the society.

Historically, housing societies and associations in England played a useful role in providing dwellings for general family letting and also for sections of the population with special needs which could not be met by the private sector. Organisations such as the Peabody Donation Fund, Rowntree Trust, Guinness Trust and Sutton Dwellings provided good accommodation at low rents for industrial workers in London and other big cities, while other associations such as the Hanover Housing Association were formed by groups of socially minded people to house old people, handicapped persons, single women, discharged prisoners and unmarried mothers.

In 1935, the National Federation of Housing Societies was formed, at the request of the Ministry of Health, to co-ordinate and make representations on behalf of a number of existing housing societies and associations, many of whom had previously been affiliated to the Garden Cities and Town Planning Association in England. The duties of the Federation consisted of helping to form new housing societies, to provide details of available financial assistance, to advise on management and administration and to provide a link with appropriate government departments.

After the passing of the 1961 Housing Act and the Housing (Scotland) Act 1962, the National Federation was made responsible for promoting a new type of housing society – a cost-rent society – designed to build houses to let without the aid of rent subsidy. A sum of £25 million of government money was made available in England for cost-rent societies, while a further £3 million was allocated to Scotland in 1962 for a similar purpose.

The Finance Act of 1963 recognised that members of approved housing societies should be given tax concessions which were similar to those already granted to owner-occupiers. This concession gave rise to the formation of co-ownership housing societies. Between 1962 and 1964, 88 housing developments, comprising 5,789 houses, were approved under the 1961 Act, while seven developments comprising 463 houses under the 1962 Act were sanctioned in Scotland.

In 1964, the National Federation ceased to function as co-ordinator for the government-sponsored cost-rent and co-ownership societies, but still retained an interest in and control over those societies and associations which were in operation before the 1961 Housing Act came into operation. Responsibility for all new cost-rent and co-ownership schemes was taken over by the Housing Corporation which was set up by the government in 1965 to stimulate the growth of the housing society movement. Its business was to encourage societies to build new houses to let at cost-rent, i.e. cost-rent societies, or for occupation on the co-operative principle of group ownership, namely co-ownership societies. The Corporation was given powers to assist these societies on legal, administrative, architectural and managerial matters and joined with established building societies in lending money to finance housing construction.

Housing societies attempt to meet the needs of a wide variety of people who may be unable or unwilling to rent or to obtain mortgages for a house. With the cost-rent society, the rent is never greater than that required to defray the cost of building, maintenance, insurance and management. Rents are not raised arbitrarily and a tenant may move at short notice. The co-ownership society asks for an initial cash outlay, which is considerably less than the deposit, legal cost, surveyors' fees, etc., which normally confront a potential owner-occupier. Societies' loans are repayable over forty years, thus resulting in smaller monthly payments by members than those paid normally to a building society by owner-occupiers. The same tax benefits are available as with conventional mortgage schemes, while the government's mortgage option scheme is also available to members of all co-ownership societies. Members of cost-rent and co-ownership societies are free from all major maintenance worries. The society handles all major repairs, insurances and the maintenance of landscaped areas and other facilities. The rent payable by the member is sufficient to discharge his shares of servicing the society's mortgages and the expenses incurred in maintaining and managing the estate as a whole.

A member of a co-ownership society is free to withdraw from the society and to move out of his house whenever he chooses by giving due notice. He has no personal liability for disposing of his house, but simply returns his agreement to the society which arranges for a new member to take over. Provided the outgoing member's rent is paid up to date and there are no outstanding charges for dilapidation or damage, he will get back his original deposit. In addition, and provided he has occupied his house for not less than three years, he is entitled to a further payment based on the amount which he has contributed to the reduction of the total capital debt and on any change which may have taken place in the value of the house during his occupation.

Co-ownership societies are suitable for single people of all ages, for young single people and for older people without capital assets; they are able to cater for many groups in society who do not fall into the preferred family categories on the local authority housing lists, or those most favoured by building societies.

Both types of society offer houses designed and constructed to good standards. Imaginative design is encouraged in the planning of the houses and in the over-all layout and appearance of developments. Social and collective responsibility is shared by all members of the society who elect a committee to run the internal affairs of the group. The committee is able to control the general appearance of the development and is responsible for all external repairs and maintenance. This is an important factor in the continuing success of many housing society developments.

In 1972, co-ownership housing was making reasonable progress in England, whereas cost-rent societies had become totally uneconomic due to spiralling building costs. In direct contrast, co-ownership housing societies had made little progress in Scotland, while the cost-rent movement made practically no impression at all.

The Housing Finance Act 1972 enabled the Housing Corporation to lend to all housing associations and not just to those societies affiliated to that organisation. Since then, the majority of the Housing Corporation loans to housing associations have been for subsidised rented housing. By 1973, new co-ownership housing had been priced out of the market by rising building costs and rising interest rates. The Housing Corporation therefore switched its main effort to lending on acquisitions, conversions and improvements to existing houses for subsidised renting purposes.

The Housing Act 1974 greatly strengthened the powers of the Housing Corporation and more than doubled its borrowing capacity. The Corporation was now given the responsibility for promoting the development of the voluntary housing movement as a whole; in addition it was empowered to buy and develop land for house-building purposes where necessary. Currently, the Corporation is concentrating on the improvement of the existing housing stock in 'stress areas' and providing housing for those in special need, i.e. handicapped persons, elderly people, single persons, large families and the ex-occupants of tied houses. In theory, the voluntary housing movement is an excellent idea and receives wide support from all sections of the community, including politicians from all political parties. The reality, however, is somewhat different and merits some explanation.

A recent quotation from an article on housing associations by John Hands, the Director of the Society for Co-operative Dwellings in London, sums up the position perfectly.

> Not only has the voluntary housing movement generally failed to be an effective force, it has failed to be a third or distinctive one. It uses the same sources of finance and largely houses the same groups of people as do the other two (local authority and private builders) and up to now it has been heavily dependent on local authorities for finance.

This quotation refers mainly to England and to London in particular. The problem faced by housing societies in Scotland is, if anything, much worse! The housing society and housing association movement was given little opportunity or incentive to develop in Scotland; few, if any, of the charitable organisations, such as the Peabody Donation Fund, have operated successfully there.

With the formation of the Scottish branch of the National Federation of Housing Societies in 1935, some improvement could be expected; very little in fact happened. Speakers at a housing conference held in Edinburgh two years later complained of a general reluctance on the part of local authorities to enter into agreements with housing associations; cases were described where applications by associations had been refused in areas of known housing shortage. In the face of this apathy and, in some cases, downright opposition, the Department of Health made little attempt to assist and encourage the voluntary housing movement in Scotland.

After the war the pattern continued, only this time the Department of Health was itself responsible for restricting the work of the associations to building houses for miners, farm servants and other key workers. Somehow, by 1951, 33 associations had come into existence; 22 were concerned with the provision of general family housing, seven with housing for old people, three for industrial workers and one for disabled ex-servicemen. Initially, the key to the problem in Scotland lay with the local authorities. They were empowered to grant financial assistance and in some cases to allocate land to the associations, providing there was satisfactory evidence of a need for houses in a given area. As far as the housing associations were concerned, there appeared to be no need for houses in many areas of Scotland during the 1950s.

This ridiculous state of affairs cannot be blamed entirely on the local authorities. Successive post-war governments were largely indifferent to housing societies and associations; they did not understand their problems and gave little thought to altering existing housing legislation which would have given the movement an opportunity to develop and to become an effective force in the housing market.

After 1969, housing societies registered with the newly formed Housing Corporation fared little better in their efforts to promote new housing developments. The problem of local authority apathy and intransigence remained; to this must be added the frustrating and stultifying bureaucracy of the Housing Corporation itself.

Housing societies have always experienced considerable difficulties in obtaining suitable land for housing development. The problem of land shortage was now compounded by a number of additional factors: no special privileges were granted to the societies by the Housing Corporation in respect of land purchase. Societies were expected to pay the district valuer's price which was always below the current market rate for land in any given area. Even when a seller of land was favourably disposed towards a society, delays in settling a district valuer's price and in receiving the necessary purchasing permissions from Whitehall meant the loss of many good sites for housing development. An ironical twist to this ridiculous position occurred recently when a housing society was offered a prime site for housing by a new-town development corporation. In this case the district valuer's selling price was the market price and was obviously in excess of the equivalent valued buying price, i.e. the purchasing price of the Housing Corporation and that of the housing society. In this instance, it may well be asked whether the government of the day was serious in its declared intention of helping the voluntary housing movement in Scotland.

Needless to say, many local authorities gave land shortage as an excuse for not helping the voluntary housing movement. And under the present legislation (pre-1974) housing societies are unable to obtain land at rates which they can afford without receiving sympathetic support from local authorities.

The financing of new housing society projects was intended to be supplied from two sources: one third of the money was to be given by the government and the remaining two thirds was to be raised from building societies. During the 1960s, the third portion allocated by the government was often not available owing to recurring economic problems both at home and abroad; the building societies experienced a series of cash-flow problems during this period and also withheld money.

They were also suspicious of new ventures which involved lending money to groups of people as opposed to traditional borrowing by individuals. Latterly, the building societies' commitment was reduced to one half; this made little difference to their lending performance or their attitude to housing societies.

Both Conservative and Labour Governments have paid cynical lip service to the voluntary housing movement in Britain as a whole and to Scotland in particular. During the 1960s, the first cuts in government expenditure, during the recurring periods of economic crisis, were borne by the housing associations and housing societies – the writer sees no reason to doubt that this pattern of priority in government housing expenditure will continue into the seventies, irrespective of how much money is allocated and regardless of who is in charge of the organisation. Neither party feels committed to or sufficiently involved with a movement which does not conform to the dreary pattern of right versus left, or private versus public sectors. The voluntary housing movement holds no special significance for politicians in Scotland.

This indifference also occurs at local level. A recent survey of local authority attitudes to housing societies varied between some knowledge, ignorance, indifference and veiled opposition. Those authorities which are ignorant of the housing society movement have some cause, in that all Scottish legislation on Housing Corporation activities is contained within English Housing Acts, whereas all references to public and private sector housing are contained in separate Scottish housing documents. Understandably, most local authorities in Scotland read the Scottish Housing Acts only. Those authorities which are opposed to the movement fall roughly into two categories: the first group still regards housing societies as potential rivals to its own house-building programmes in the public sector. It realises that it cannot control rents or manage houses built by housing societies; this does not conform to its concept of social housing managed by paternalistic authority. The second group does not want to encourage housing societies, fearing that building work and building land may be taken from private house builders in its district. Both groups are suspicious of the voluntary housing movement and seem ready to quote isolated cases of incompetence or bad management.

The Scottish division of the Housing Corporation is not entirely blameless in this matter. Official Housing Corporation policy during the late 1960s was to discourage the formation of additional housing societies. Existing smaller groups were encouraged to join with larger groups, presumably to promote greater efficiency and to simplify the work of the Corporation. This 'bureaucratic tidying' completely negated the spirit behind the voluntary housing movement and did little to further housing society activities in Scotland. Surrounded by indifference and in some cases animosity, the Corporation adopted a negative stance and while it is readily admitted that some of the developments built were attractive, interesting and relatively advanced in concept, it is clear that the over-all performance by the Scottish division during the recent past was very poor indeed.

Table 8.1 gives an indication of the performance by the Scottish region as compared with other areas in Britain.

Table 8.1:   Total Projects Completed as at March 1973

Region	Year of Completion					Total
	1965-9	1970	1971	1972	1973	1965-73
South East	4,529	1,965	981	1,735	1,247	10,457
Wales (after 1972– Wales and Severnside)	431	36	—	—	259	726
West (after 1972– South West)	979	282	—	—	315	1,576
Midlands	2,186	1,296	624	1,676	746	6,528
Northern	2,347	1,681	270	2,510	713	7,521
Scotland	203	239	90	488	315	1,335

Note: During the period 1971-2 the boundaries between the Welsh and the South West regions appeared to have been changed. It is difficult therefore to maintain continuity of completion figures during this time.

From the table it is obvious that the number of projects completed by the Scottish region compares very unfavourably with those produced by the other regions.

To the problem of poor performance in the recent past must be added the suspicion that a government agency is by nature inevitably inflexible, bureaucratic and cannot act as an effective force to the voluntary housing movement. A committed agency appreciates that every housing society is a special case; that societies building small numbers of houses are preferred to large bureaucratically packaged developments, that a full range of conventional and unconventional building groups should be supported. It must recognise that mistakes – possibly even costly mistakes – will be made while these groups are gaining expertise in building and in management control. The neglect of the housing society movement by successive British governments over a long period of time cannot be compensated by the development of instant expertise and efficiency on the part of the newly formed housing societies and associations in the 1970s.

The Housing Corporation has already gained expertise in cost-rent and co-ownership societies which are mainly concerned with the construction of new housing; the organisation is currently grappling with the problems of rehabilitation of older housing. Has it the adaptability and flexibility required to accommodate the problems and requirements of people who want to build/rehabilitate their own homes (self-build groups are now officially recognised by the Corporation) or of organisations of tradesmen who wish to build houses for others (worker-control groups)? Can it allow for groups which do not subscribe to the conventional indicative cost of housing, and which may wish to build to lower or even to higher standards? Or again, can it lend support to persons wishing to live in community groups and who may wish to build completely unconventional house plans? In other words, should the Housing Corporation be able to support valid housing projects which presently cannot readily attract money from existing conventional government or market sources? The 1974 Housing Act has given the housing association movement a boost both in moral and in financial terms; Lord Goodman, a former chairman of the Housing Corporation, apparently committed the Corporation to the idea of reducing bureaucratic and time-wasting procedures to a minimum. Both of the major political parties appear to support the main terms of the Act in principle. The Scottish section of the Corporation has recently been placed under new management. The direction and accent of housing activity in Scotland has been altered in favour of the improvement and upgrading of existing property. This is admirable. It is certainly regretted, however, that new house building by co-ownership housing societies has been curtailed, particularly in Scotland, where these groups have never been given a fair chance to operate effectively in the period before the passing of the 1974 Act.

9 POSSIBILITIES FOR THE FUTURE

In 1973, a number of local authorities were able to report that house waiting lists were minimal and that the housing problem in their area was virtually 'solved'. Some were concerned with 'mopping up operations', while others believed their function could be safely confined to providing housing for special categories of family within the community. In the absence of a national survey of housing needs, little can be said to support or to disagree with these assessments of local housing situations.

In Aberdeen and Edinburgh local authority housing lists are numbered in thousands, while Glasgow still has over 30,000 applications for housing. On Clydeside there are many houses which are still below the official tolerable standard. In parts of the Central Lowlands, the Highlands and the Borders, isolated areas still have serious housing problems. Oil-related development in north-east Scotland has created its own particular kind of housing problem, while rising inflation is beginning to affect some sections in the community which might not normally expect to have difficulty in finding a place to live.

Under present social and economic conditions, the solution to housing problems in Scotland is not a short-term matter — something which can be solved by 1980 or 1990. Despite what may be said to the contrary, the housing problem will continue to be a permanent feature of Scottish life into the foreseeable future.

Local and national politicians will no doubt offer their own particular brands of salvation; predictably, they will offer to build more housing in the public sector, or more private housing, according to political inclination; they will inevitably promise to build x number of houses in y number of years; they will pledge increased support for housing associations and inevitably withhold finance during recurring periods of financial and economic crisis. The value of their proposals is immediately suspect in that they are saddled with the dead weight of party politics, which has distorted housing policies and programmes in Scotland for far too long.

So far, official housing policies and programmes in Scotland have been intolerably bureaucratic, highly restrictive and overtly paternalistic in character; they have failed to solve existing housing problems and are currently creating new areas of distress. Scotland has never enjoyed a coherent, appropriate or particularly humane housing policy. The end

124

product of many recent Scottish housing programmes represents a very poor investment for the future.

Having said this, is it possible to respond positively and objectively to this difficult, highly controversial and seemingly intractable problem? The writer hesitates to offer ready-made solutions, but would like to suggest some ideas – none of which is particularly new – for discussion and debate amongst those who have an interest and a commitment to the improvement of housing conditions and housing design in Scotland. For purposes of discussion, three phases of development are visualised – short-term, transitional and long-term.

Short-term Phase

The short-term phase is an emergency situation – a wartime situation – and should be recognised as such. It is hypocritical to suggest that the present housing situation on Clydeside is less than this! Special funds are required to alleviate the problem. The existing bureaucratic housing procedures should be vastly simplified or even bypassed altogether. The latter suggestion is a serious proposition and one which deserves careful and sympathetic consideration.

It is suggested that a series of shops – rather like emergency first-aid posts – be set up in the disaster areas. These shops would be permanently staffed by long-suffering sympathetic persons – preferably locals – who know the district and are genuinely interested in helping with local housing problems. Local people would be encouraged to come forward and talk about housing needs and difficulties. People with housing problems do not automatically join a council housing list or necessarily appreciate what options and alternatives might be made available to them. Many assume, and with good reason, that they have no choice in the matter. Opinions would be asked and noted so that an individual and an over-all picture of housing needs could be built up in each local district. The formation of local housing associations would be encouraged and directed initially from the 'shop'. These associations could be quite small and might be disbanded on completion of a particular project or projects.

The idea of popular involvement should not be discounted or despised – politicians, local representatives and local officials are particularly guilty of adopting this attitude. People should be encouraged to help to solve their own housing problems. A wide range of talents and skills are available in many of the distressed areas; unemployed people, school-leavers and students could also provide valuable practical assistance in local housing projects, provided the trade union movement adopted a more realistic and flexible attitude to labour relations in respect of self-help/ self-build projects. The excellent work done by 'Shelter' merits recognition and non-bureaucratic financial support. This organisation has developed considerable expertise in the emergency housing field and could provide valuable advice and assistance in many areas where severe localised housing problems exist.

The recent 'Assist Project' in Govan, Glasgow, provides a valuable object lesson in client participation and rehabilitation for tenement housing. A great deal could be done to alleviate housing problems in the older areas on Clydeside if groups such as Assist were formed and given maximum encouragement to rehabilitate existing tenement housing. The success of these proposals naturally presupposes minimal interference from local and national bureaucratic institutions.

It must be accepted that popular involvement in housing construction will create problems and mistakes will be made before expertise is gained. A system which involves participation is often abused initially, but is, in the end, more likely to produce results which satisfy immediate needs and expectations in housing disaster areas. It is emphasised that bureaucratic systems—especially those connected with social housing provision—are also abused and that this abuse is often more subtle, more dishonest and, in the end, more easily concealed from public scrutiny.

Housing programmes in the 1950s and 1960s were obviously concerned with the construction of new housing on greenfield sites or with demolition and rebuilding within existing urban areas. More recently the emphasis has shifted in favour of the rehabilitation of the older tenement properties. Officially these activities are seen as completely separate operations. Many urban areas would benefit enormously from a policy which would combine new house building and rehabilitation work within a single contract. The application of this policy at local centres in the older urban areas would raise morale and encourage local communities to think positively about urban renewal. Rehabilitation projects do little to solve the problem of 'urban blight' created by demolished gap sites. Current official attitudes positively discourage successful solutions in this highly critical area of housing design.

Transitional Phase

A prerequisite for success in the transitional period would be to extract a commitment from politicians to stop playing party politics with housing policies and programmes. The writer can think of no better recipe for early success in this respect—this would also have the added advantage of costing very little, and should thus appeal to some sections of the political community.

A Scottish Housing Board would be set up to administer a coherent and hopefully an appropriate housing policy for Scotland. The organisation would be staffed by people with a commitment to the idea of helping the people of Scotland to help themselves to better housing. The existing bureaucratic process would be progressively dismantled, blanket indicative costs and cost ratio densities, building and highway regulations and all the other ridiculous paraphernalia would be altered in favour of a freer attitude to housing policies and to housing design.

The first task of the Housing Board would be to sponsor a national survey of housing need in Scotland. This survey is obviously necessary and would form the basis for a sensible and realistic housing policy. The survey would include amongst other things total numbers actually housed, total numbers inadequately housed, or homeless, the rate and projected rate of family formation, variation in family sizes, projected new housing construction rate, rehabilitation and demolition rates. Employment trends would also have to be carefully considered, both at local and at national level. The Board would also sponsor a survey of land ownership in the urban and surrounding areas. This survey anticipates a time in which all urban land will be owned by local communities.

The Board would also be faced with the problem of housing promotion and tenure. Who should promote new housing groups in Scotland and what new forms of tenure should be established in addition to traditional methods of occupancy? Encouragement should be given to groups which offer maximum choice. People should be allowed to choose the house and method of tenure from a series of reasonable housing options. These options would range from renting to complete self-help/self-build schemes. There are many models and many precedents in other European countries which could be adapted to suit local conditions in Scotland.

A variety of housing associations and housing co-operatives would be formed to augment the work of the existing non-profit-making housing groups. It is important that these groups do not expand unnecessarily and thus run the risk of becoming top-heavy and excessively bureaucratic in character. The writer believes that small housing groups provide the best opportunity to meet the varied needs of society as a whole.

It is perhaps self-evident that problems of financing housing in Scotland arise largely because society cannot find any socially acceptable method of keeping the capital value of housing within the rent or mortgage repayment capacity of a large number of families. It follows from this that the supply of capital and the co-ordination of all housing subsidies must become an integral part of a comprehensive housing policy. Existing taxation policies and housing policies are strictly compartment-alised despite the fact that taxation plays a vital role in housing econ-omics and also in housing subsidies.

The present distorted and inadequate system of housing subsidies – all housing subsidies in Britain seem to have come into existence through accidents of history – should be abandoned in favour of an equitable system which treats all tenure groups, owner-occupiers, council and housing association tenants with equal consideration. The new subsidy would form an integral part of a revised income tax system. Subsidies could be allocated in the form of a reduction in income tax. Persons not paying income tax would receive a subsidy payment in lieu of tax rebate. The subsidy would be administered through local income tax offices.

Capital investment in housing also presents a problem not only in Scotland, but for all western democracies. It has already been noted that successive British governments have frequently denied resources for necessary housing development in Scotland. In the present econ-omic climate, it is difficult to see how the government could be per-suaded to make additional monies available for housing. It is, perhaps, time to persuade private financial institutions to direct a percentage of their vast assets into housing investment. Insurance companies, com-mercial banks and investment trusts are not noted for philanthropic endeavour. They do, however, enjoy a highly privileged position in soc-iety and could reasonably be expected to invest in subsidised housing development. The writer would regard this as a test of social respons-ibility on the part of these organisations.

Building societies have always taken a rather negative attitude to lending money for housing in Scotland; they are excessively concerned with security of investment and are extremely cautious in their dealings with 'unconventional' borrowers. This attitude creates problems for independent housing groups, housing societies and other groups who require to borrow money for housing development on a group basis. Excessive caution on the part of the building societies positively assists deterioration and the creation of blighted housing areas within the older parts of many burghs and cities. Young persons – and the not-so-young – are dissuaded from buying houses because they are often unable to obtain loans for properties within these inner areas. There is also still a suspicion, despite assurances to the contrary, that many people are not eligible or acceptable for building society loans. This may equally apply to new and to older properties. Again, it seems fair and reasonable to expect building societies to act in a socially responsible manner towards the community as a whole.

Since the trade union movement in Britain decided to invest in equity shares at the beginning of the 1960s, it might also be reasonable to expect this organisation to invest money in housing development. It was also suggested in an earlier chapter that the building trade unions could take a positive and active role in housing promotion and construction. This in itself presupposes active financial commitment to house-building activity.

The reorganisation and liberalisation of building, planning and high-way regulations should help designers to improve housing layouts and house designs. It is also up to designers to raise their own standards, to be more ambitious in housing design, to be more demanding of them-selves and to appreciate that housing design is an important, desirable and worthwhile problem. Younger architects are beginning to appreciate the folly of building large impersonal housing developments for large numbers of unknown and under-privileged clients. In this respect, they are becoming more aware and more sensitive to the legitimate needs of others. Hopefully, the dangerous megalomania which gripped so many housing designers of public sector housing in the 1960s is now a thing of the past. History must surely record this decade as one of the most dismal periods in Scottish housing development during the twentieth century.

Existing financial constraints will inevitably overlap into the housing economics of the transitional period. Substantial savings are now all but impossible to obtain in low-cost housing. It is simply nonsense to expect housing designers in Scotland to reduce the area of inadequate house plans or to produce miraculous specifications, which produce significant cost reductions.

In the public sector Scotland officially receives a higher allocation of money per house than England and Wales. Evidence suggests, however, that a much higher proportion is required to give a comparable standard of house. This differential is most noticeable when comparisons are made with housing developments in the south-east of England where the standard of materials, finish and external works appears to be of a much higher order.

New technologies in housing design are obviously possible, but these cannot initially produce economies in housing design. The production of the heavy, inflexible, factory-produced housing systems in the 1960s underlines the fallacy of believing that there might be one big techno-logical solution to housing problems.

Moves towards the creation of a sensitive domestic environment in the transitional period presupposes that a number of Scottish housing shibboleths will have to be overturned. It also follows that attitudes to housing design will undergo significant change. The housing designer would in certain cases assume the role of 'family doctor' as opposed to 'remote consultant' in matters concerned with house design and house layout. He might operate from a corner shop or from small local offices, or even act as a travelling consultant to local housing associations. He would act as an involved and committed adviser and not as a detached manipulator; he should also be prepared to interpret the needs of a variety of conventional and unconventional housing groups. Official Housing Board policy would support this form of housing 'back-up' design service.

Smaller housing developments would be preferred to large impersonal housing schemes. The rehabilitation and restoration of older domestic property would continue to play a significant role in transitional housing programmes. New housing designs would allow for built-in flexibility to enable occupiers to add to, subtract from and alter accommodation according to their needs and requirements. Rigid 'official' housing plans would have limited application and little significance in transitional housing programmes.

Official Housing Board policy would also encourage the production of well-designed, adaptable building components from a range of traditional and non-traditional materials for housing construction. Housing research and development would also play a significant part in Housing Board policy. Housing management would also be given greater emphasis and greater priority by the Housing Board. Considerable expertise would be required to administer new housing societies and associations sponsored by the Board and other organisations.

The Housing Board would also make a very positive effort to promote and encourage housing competitions to stimulate better housing design both at local and at national level. Housing competitions both at national and at local level hardly exist in Scotland and of the very few competitions held since 1950, the prize winners displayed a very modest level of expectation and achievement.

Long-term Phase

In the long term, housing requirements are difficult to forecast. Much will depend on population trends and employment prospects. Notwithstanding, housing 'need' will probably be replaced by housing 'demand'; this change will have to be appreciated by housing designers and other groups concerned with housing development. The Housing Board would continue to operate policies and programmes which offer maximum flexibility and choice to individuals. Home ownership will probably become the most sought-after form of housing tenure.

In this period, all urban land and land in the surrounding urban areas would be administered by local communities. Methods of sponsorship and tenure may become even more varied. For example, groups of people may opt for more communal forms of living, which may radically alter expected housing requirements. It is also anticipated that many more people will be interested in self-build housing. Housing designers must be prepared to respond to changing attitudes, to changing domestic organisation and to changing sponsors and builders.

It is difficult to foresee a situation in which the supply of housing finance will be organised on a fair and rational basis—a basis in which all groups in society have an opportunity to obtain and to live in decent accommodation. In a more equitable society, methods of financing housing will have to be radically altered—excessive usury cannot be regarded forever as a suitable financial regulator. It also follows from this that individuals must look to their own priorities and responsibilities in matters concerned with the financing of housing.

In the long term housing design can only reflect social attitudes and conditions in society. Hopefully, this society will be both individually and collectively more humane, more socially responsible and certainly more responsive to the individual and his requirements. The housing designer should be in a position to respond to this challenge with equal humanity and responsibility.

INDEX

Aberdeen 14, 29, 124
access roads 97, 102, 106, 111
Annual Bulletin of Housing Statistics 34, 85, 87
ARAVA 60
architectural competitions 35, 54
architects 72, 73, 76, 80, 99, 101, 102, 103, 104, 107, 108, 111, 129
Argyll, Duke of 18
Assist project 126
ASUNTOSAATAJAT 59
Austria 34

backlands 15, 16, 20
Ballikinrain mill 18
banks 43, 60, 61, 128
Barlow Commission 111, 112
Bearsden, Glasgow 30
Belgium 33, 35-8
Berlin, West 43
Blackhall, Edinburgh 30
Blythswood 20
Board of Health 28
building and highway regulations 24, 103, 104, 105, 127, 129
building industry, drawbacks 107-9
building societies 30, 31, 34, 38, 120, 121, 128-9
Building Standards Regulations (Scotland) 105
building trade unions 63, 64, 109, 110, 111, 129
Bulgaria 34
bungalows 30
bureaucracy 124, 125, 126, 127
Burghs of Barony 14, 15

Canmore, Malcolm 14
Carntyne, Glasgow 28, 29
car parks 105
Catrine village 18
Central Lowlands 19, 97, 124
choice, in housing 33, 71-3, 81, 82, 89, 110, 115
City Improvement Act 22
Clydeside 95, 124, 125, 126
Cockburn, John 18

commercial development 67
community services 29, 48
Conservative Party housing policy 84, 121
co-ownership housing societies 116, 117, 118, 123
Copenhagen 23, 54
cost-rent housing societies 116, 117, 118, 123
council housing 33, 56, 68-83 *passim*; *see also* public sector housing
County Board 64, 65
Craig, James 16
credit societies 23
Crieff 18
Cumbernauld 114
Czechoslovakia 34

Dale, David 18
David I, King 14
daylighting 105, 111
Deanston village 18
decay, areas in 112, 113
delayed sale 47
delaying tactics in building 104
Denmark 23, 49, 51, 54-8
Department of Health 28, 119
deterioration in housing 77-8
disabled ex-servicemen, housing for 119
discharged pensioners, housing for 116
Dundee 26, 29

East Kilbride 114
economic regulator, building industry as 108
Edinburgh 14, 16, 22, 23, 24, 25, 26, 29, 30, 124; new town 16, 17
Edinburgh Co-operative Building Company Ltd 23
England, housing standards 26, 32, 33
Essex County Council 102
European Economic Community (EEC) 32, 33, 35
Europe, Eastern 33, 34

ex-occupants of tied houses, housing
for 118

factory villages 18
Fairmilehead, Edinburgh 30
Falkland 18
family allowances 47
family housing 44, 118, 119
farm servants, housing for 119
farmtoun settlements 13, 15, 17, 19
feus 20, 22, 25
Finland 49, 51, 58-61
Finnish Family Welfare League
(VAESTOLIITTO) 59
First World War 26, 55
fixed price contracts 108
flats 16, 19, 21, 22, 23, 34, 35, 44,
62, 66, 76
Fochabers 18
France 32, 33, 35, 46-7
free sector housing 42

Garden Cities and Town Planning
Association 116
garden cities, gardens 23, 28, 45,
114
Germany, West 32, 33, 34, 42-6
Ginsburgh, Leslie 106
Glasgow 19, 22, 25, 26, 27, 28, 29,
30, 83, 124
Glasgow Workmen's Dwelling Com-
pany 23
Glenrothes 114
Goodman, Lord 107, 123
Gorbals 20
Govan, Glasgow 126
government, and housing policy 26,
27, 30, 31, 33, 34, 59, 73, 84,
85, 93, 95, 120, 121, 123, 128
Government Housing Act 68
Granton 18
Greve, Prof. John 54, 85
group ownership 35, 83
Guiness Trust 116

Habitations à Loyer Modéré (HLM) 46,
47
Hamburg 44
handicapped people, housing for
116, 118
Hands, John 119
Hanover Housing Association 116
Helsinki 60
Helsinki Central Housing Society

(HAKA) 59
high-rise building 16, 66, 76, 77
History of Working-Class Housing 20
house completions 84, 85, 89, 92, 96
house prices 28, 97, 100, 101
house sizes 66, 84-5
House, Town Planning (Scotland) Act
(Addison Act) 26, 27
Housing Act: 1920 27; 1923 27, 68;
1924 (Wheatly Act) 27, 28; 1961
116, 117; 1969 78; 1974 118,
123
Housing Act (Netherlands) 39
Housing Acts (Belgium) 36-8
Housing Acts (Germany) 43-4
housing allocations 80-2
housing associations/societies 12,
31, 33, 34, 35, 36, 39, 40, 41, 42,
43, 44, 52, 54, 55, 56, 57, 59, 60,
64, 77, 78, 89, 92, 116-23, 125,
127, 128
Housing Board Act (Finland) 60
Housing Board, proposed 127, 130,
131
Housing Code (Belgium) 38
housing committees 69, 70, 72, 73
housing companies 43, 44
housing co-operatives 12, 23, 24, 33,
34, 45, 46, 47, 52, 54, 55, 58,
59, 60, 61, 62, 63, 64, 83, 127
Housing Corporation 107, 117, 118,
120, 121, 122, 123
housing costs 27, 28, 47, 75, 77,
101, 102, 104, 106, 107, 123,
127
housing debt 92, 93
housing density 26, 27, 72, 105, 106,
111, 114-23
housing design and layout 12, 28, 32,
39, 48, 50, 72, 97, 98, 100, 101,
102, 103, 105, 106, 107, 111,
115, 118, 129, 130, 131
Housing Finance Act 118
Housing Foundation (ASUNTOSAATIC)
59
Housing in the Nordic Countries 52
housing lists 80, 81, 82, 124
housing maintenance and management 82, 110, 118
Housing of the Working Classes Act
25
housing returns 82
Housing Scotland Act: 1930 (Greenwood Act) 29; 1935 29; 1949 71;

1962 116
housing standards 32, 42, 84, 85, 89,
    94, 106, 123, 124
housing subsidies 27, 28, 29, 30, 36,
    37, 39, 41, 43, 53, 57, 58, 60, 61,
    62, 64, 65, 66, 67, 76, 84, 92, 93,
    94, 128
Housing Subsidy Act (Denmark) 55
Howard, Ebenezer 111
Hungary 34

indicative costs 75, 77, 106, 107,
    108, 123, 127
industrialised housing 57, 59, 129
industrial workers, housing for 119
institutional investors (Netherlands)
    39, 40, 41
insurance companies 40, 43, 46, 64,
    128
interest rates, on housing loans 40,
    41, 60, 65, 92
Inveraray 18
investment companies 40, 128
Ireland 85
Irvine 114
Italy 32, 33

joint stock associations 56, 59

Kirkcudbright 18
Knightswood, Glasgow 28

Labour Party, housing policy 84, 121
land 22, 45, 66, 70, 71, 74, 96, 103,
    105, 118, 120, 131; costs 40, 97,
    101
landscaping 27, 28, 30, 42, 97, 117
Lawrie brothers 20
Letchworth Garden City 27, 111
Livingstone 114
local authorities, and housing 11, 25,
    27, 28, 31, 33, 42, 59, 68-83, 89,
    92, 106, 107, 108, 109, 110, 119,
    120, 121, 124
location, of housing 71, 72
London 16, 95
lower income groups, housing for
    33, 44, 45, 47, 53, 55, 68, 71,
    92, 110, 111

Malmö 66
market research, in housing 98, 99
miners, housing for 21, 26, 36, 119
mortgage banks 64

mortgage companies 46, 47
mortgages 36, 41, 44, 60, 61, 64, 65,
    66, 93, 117
Moss Park, Glasgow 27
motivation, in housing 73-4
municipalities 39, 41, 42, 53, 54, 59,
    60, 61, 62, 64, 66; *see also* local
    authorities

National Federation of Housing Soc-
    ieties 116, 117, 119
National Housing Account (Belgium)
    36
National Housing Board (Finland) 60,
    61
National Housing Institute (Belgium)
    35, 37
National Housing Society (Belgium)
    35, 37, 38
National Landed Property Society
    (Belgium) 38
National Rural Property Society
    (Belgium) 35
Netherlands 32, 33, 39-42
Neue Heimat 44, 45-6; Kommunal
    45
New Lanark 18
Newton Mearns, Glasgow 30
new towns 16, 17, 33, 102, 111-12,
    114-15; Act 112; Committee 111;
    development corporations 114,
    120
Norway 49, 51

old people, housing for 40, 46, 116,
    118, 119
Ormiston 18
overcrowding 11, 13, 20, 21, 22, 24,
    26, 29, 64, 66, 77, 95
Owen, Robert 18
owner-occupation 31, 33, 34, 35, 36,
    40, 41, 42, 43, 44, 89, 93, 96,
    115, 116, 128, 131

package deals, by builders 75, 76,
    77
Paisley 29
party politics, and housing 31, 73,
    74, 84, 85, 110, 121, 124, 126
paternalism, in housing 18, 78-80, 82,
    110
Peabody Donation Fund 116, 119
pension funds 37, 40
permissions, building 74-6, 104

personal loans 60, 61
Perth, Duke of 18
planning 72, 73, 76, 80, 99, 100,
  101, 102, 103-15, 129; code 111;
  committees 73
Poland 34
Portugal 85, 86
pre-fabricated houses 57
private building 11-12, 30, 31, 33,
  39, 41, 42, 43, 46, 54, 59, 60,
  61, 62, 64, 65, 89, 96-102
problem families 29
promotion, in housing 68-70, 127
property-specific loans 60, 61
public offices 46, 47
public sector housing 11, 33, 34, 35,
  46, 68-83, 84, 87, 89, 92, 96,
  102, 107, 108, 115, 129
public services 102, 103, 104
public utility companies 61, 62, 64
Public Works Loan Board 92
purchase-sale promise system 38

rates, local 27, 77, 92, 93
reciprocal loans 61
rehabilitation of older housing 77,
  78, 123, 126, 130
Reith, Lord 111
rent 24, 27; control 26, 77; rebates
  43; subsidies 57, 58, 65
rented housing 25, 27, 28, 29, 30,
  35, 41, 42, 44, 45, 47, 56, 59,
  60, 64, 68-83, 89, 96, 115, 118,
  127
repayment, on housing loans 65, 66,
  92
roads and highways 97, 104, 105,
  106
Romania 34
Rothschild, Lord 87
Rowntree Trust 116
Royal Burghs 14-15
Royal Commission on housing 11,
  26, 27
rural societies (Belgium) 36

sanitation 16, 21, 25, 33
SATO organisation 59
savings banks 36, 37, 40, 47, 64
Scandinavia 12, 23, 48-67, 109, 110
Scotland, housing standards 32, 33,
  42, 48, 49, 51
Scottish Development Department
  72, 74, 75, 77, 82, 104, 105

Scottish Housing Advisory Committee
  11, 97
segregation, in housing 45, 70-1, 82
self-build housing 79, 123, 126, 127,
  131
Shelter 82, 126
shops, housing advice centres 125
Sidwell, Prof. 97
single persons, housing for 116, 118
slum clearance 28, 29, 36, 38
social benefit associations 56
social housing 35, 36, 37, 38, 43, 44,
  46, 109, 110
social integration 16, 34, 47, 48, 58-9,
  70
Society for Co-operative Dwellings
  119
space, in housing 32, 42, 48, 97, 111
speculation 20, 22, 24, 25, 26, 27,
  30, 45, 70, 76-7, 111
SSHA 33
Stanley village 18
status seeking, by Britain 51, 52,
  86-7
Stirling 14, 16, 29
Stockholm 62, 66
stone, building in 15, 18, 27, 29
students, housing for 46
Summerston, Glasgow 83
Sutton Dwellings 116
Svenska Bostäder 61
Svenska Rikbyggen (SR) 52, 63, 64
Sweden 49, 51, 61-6, 67
Swedish Confederation of Trade
  Unions 64

Tapiola 59
taxation 25, 128; concessions 36, 43,
  47, 93, 116, 128
Taylor, Nicholas 72
Tayside 113
tenants' associations 56, 79, 83
Tenants Savings and Building Society
  (HSB) 62, 63, 64
tenements 15, 16, 21, 22, 23, 24, 25,
  26, 27, 70, 77, 126
tenure 33, 35, 47, 72, 82, 83, 89,
  110, 115, 127, 131
trade unions 44, 45, 46, 52, 56, 59,
  63, 64, 109, 110, 111, 125, 129
Treasury 75, 104, 106, 107
Tudor Walter Committee 111

unemployment 51, 57, 63, 95

unmarried mothers, housing for 116
urban renewal and redevelopment
    45, 113, 126
USSR 34

Vällingby 62
vandalism 49
VATRO (joint stock company) 59
village communities 17-18
Village in the City 72
villas 19, 30, 70
Voluntary Housing in Scandinavia 54
voluntary housing movement 12, 118,
    119, 121, 122
VVO (housing co-operative society)
    59

West Central Scotland Planning Com-
    mittee 94
worker controlled building groups 54,
    55, 110-11, 123
Workers' Building Association 54
Workers' Co-operative Building
    Association 55
Workers' Co-operative Housing
    Association 55
working class housing 21, 23, 24, 25,
    26, 27, 29, 32, 33, 36

Yorkshire 96, 97
young married couples, housing for
    46
Yugoslavia 34